In Retrospect:
The History of a Historian

Other Books by Arthur M. Schlesinger

AUTHOR

The Colonial Merchants and the American Revolution, 1763-1776. 1918.

New Viewpoints in American History. 1922.

Political and Social History of the United States, 1829-1925. 1925. Revised editions, 1933, 1941.

The Rise of the City, 1878-1898. 1933.

Learning How to Behave, a Historical Study of American Etiquette Books. 1946.

Paths to the Present. 1949. Revised edition, 1963.

The American as Reformer. 1950.

The Rise of Modern America, 1865-1951. 1951.

Prelude to Independence: The Newspaper War on Britain, 1764-1776. 1958.

CO-AUTHOR

The Reinterpretation of American Literature. 1928.

Research in the Social Sciences. 1929.

Essays on Research in the Social Sciences. 1931.

Approaches to American Social History. 1937.

Land of the Free, a Short History of the American People. 1944.

Harvard Guide to American History. 1954.

EDITOR

Great Charters of Americanism. 1920.

Historical Scholarship in America: Needs and Opportunities. 1932.

Marcus Lee Hansen, *The Atlantic Migration, 1607-1860.* 1940.

Marcus Lee Hansen, *The Immigrant in American History.* 1940.

Frederick Law Olmsted, *The Cotton Kingdom.* 1953.

CO-EDITOR

A History of American Life. 13 vols. 1927-1948.

In Retrospect:
The History of a Historian

Arthur M. Schlesinger

Harcourt, Brace & World, Inc.
New York

FOR
MY SONS
ARTHUR AND THOMAS

Preface

The men and women of my generation have lived through a remarkable epoch in the history of America as well as of the world. Since 1888, when I was born, the republic has grown from thirty-eight to fifty states, including two apart from the central core; the population has trebled; a predominantly rural country has become predominantly urban and industrial; the state and national governments have unprecedentedly extended their powers to further the general welfare; the American people have attained the closest ever known to a classless society; and mechanical inventions such as the automobile, airplane, movie, radio, and television have transformed life at all levels, with the climactic harnessing of nuclear energy holding forth untold benefits or total extinction for civilization. In the same span of years the United States in its overseas relations abandoned its traditional policy of nonentanglement to join twice with freedom-loving countries in waging desperate war against deadly threats to the democratic form of government, and it ended by being the leader and mainstay of an international organization to promote peace, self-rule, and justice for all mankind. In terms also of towering figures the period has been exceptional. In the political field, for good or ill, such men have stood forth as the two Roosevelts, Wilson, Churchill, and Gandhi, on the one hand, and Lenin, Mussolini, Hitler, and Stalin, on the other, while in the advancement of knowledge the era has produced such giants as Freud and Jung, Pavlov, Cannon, Einstein, and Rutherford.

The life of an age inescapably enters in some degree into the life of each individual. This memoir attests one man's reactions to the times, though as a teacher and writer of American history I was mainly an observer of great events, seldom an actor in them. After a sketch of childhood and college days these pages deal largely with academic affairs and personalities in three universities and, particularly, with the altered character of historical study in my years. Such matters, however, as will be evident, were constantly affected by the currents of social, political, and economic change.

This book originated in a series of tape-recorded interviews conducted for the Oral History Research Office at Columbia University by Dr. Saul Benison, now of Brandeis University. In preparing the memoir for publication considerable detail concerning my professional activities has been omitted. My wife and son Arthur gave me the benefit of their criticisms, and my secretary, Elizabeth F. Hoxie, also helped materially at many points. None of these, however, bears any responsibility for the opinions expressed.

Cambridge, Massachusetts
June 1, 1963

Contents

In Retrospect:
The History of a Historian

I

Growing Up

Someone, perhaps it was Mark Twain, observed that when he was young most of what he remembered was true but that when older most of what he remembered was untrue. To describe the little Midwestern town in which I was born I have therefore drawn heavily on the thumbnail sketch I wrote in the *History of American Life* thirty years ago.

Xenia with its seven or eight thousand inhabitants was the county seat of a thriving rural community in southwestern Ohio. Maples and elms shaded the wide, macadamized streets laid out at right angles. Behind red brick walks and neat picket fences there stood modest houses where grown-ups, rocking on their porches on summer evenings, visited with each other. Deep back yards, containing a fruit tree or so and perhaps a chicken coop and a barn, provided elbow room for the children to play, the rear gates opening onto a lane of beckoning adventure, known to prosaic elders as "th' alley." The people's morals were safeguarded less by the single blue-uniformed policeman or the lively concern signified by the dozen church steeples than by the intimate knowledge everyone had of everyone else's affairs.

3

Signs abounded of the vital role of the horse. A hitching post marked the curb of virtually every dwelling and place of business, while rusting iron troughs offered drinking water at important street corners. A store with a huge dapple-gray wooden Percheron in front sold harness, and blacksmith shops —dark caverns of enchantment to juveniles—replaced the animals' lost or worn-out shoes. To accommodate the Xenian who lacked his own horse and buggy a half-dozen livery stables were at hand. I do not remember seeing an automobile until I was twelve or thirteen. The early ones were too expensive, as well as extremely noisy and balky to operate. It took some years and better and cheaper cars before the "horseless carriage" assumed command.

Except for a few outlying small mills for the manufacture of paper, rope, and footwear, the business activity centered at the intersection of Main and Detroit Streets. There, in a setting of lawn and trees, the weather-battered stone courthouse bearing aloft the town clock dominated the surroundings, with a bandstand and hitching rails in the rear. There, too, within a few minutes' walk, stood the lawyers' offices and the principal retail establishments: the groceries and butcher shops, which during the hunting season displayed skinned rabbits that looked disturbingly like dead cats; the drygoods and clothing stores; the barbershops with their striped red-and-white poles; the drugstore exhibiting great bottles of colored liquid in its windows; and the cigar store with its impassive wooden Indian on guard. Close by rose the only other civic edifice, a brick structure with corner pinnacles and tall pointed tower called the opera house. Though the name was too pretentious, it did contain an auditorium for lectures and theatrical entertainments. Its main function, however, was to house the municipal offices and the jail. Nearby, too, the Xenia *Gazette*, the only daily paper, was published, and the public library occupied a large upstairs room of a business building. Twice a day the Little Miami railway train puffed and clanged through the section, its 8:30 whistle in the evening acting as an unofficial curfew for the small fry.

For six days of the week life ran on an even keel, but on Saturday the streets took on a great stir and bustle, for then the country people hitched up Nelly or Dobbin and thronged into Xenia: bearded oldsters self-conscious in their Sunday "best"; teen-aged swains squiring bashful sweethearts; thin-chested mothers herding restless broods. It was a welcome break in the routine of the farmers and their families, a time of hard work and many sales for the shopkeepers.

The townsfolk came predominantly of old American stock. The name Xenia (from the Greek for "hospitality") harked back to its founding in 1803, when New England settlers faring into western New York and the new state of Ohio dotted the map with such reminders of classical antiquity as Troy, Athens, Rome, and Utica. In the mid-century and later, small groups direct from Europe appeared on the scene, first Germans, then Irishmen. The Germans, who scattered widely through the city, generally made their living as storekeepers. The Irish, clustered in the West End near the single Catholic church and the parochial grade school, worked for the most part in the factories.

There were, besides, a considerable number of Negroes in a neighborhood to themselves in the East End, whence the men and women went forth each morning to labor at unskilled jobs and domestic service. They comprised a quarter of the population, and a favorite jest of my boyhood attributed their presence to a wreck on the Underground Railroad. Though the progeny of escaped slaves did account for some, actually the first arrivals had been Negroes whom tender-hearted Southern planters had emancipated and sent north. An orderly element, they possessed their own churches and public educational system through the high school. This was not due, however, to legal compulsion but to geographical convenience. In my graduating class in the "white" high school were two colored girls who had attended from outside the district. I was never aware of any feeling against the race, only of one of sympathy for their poverty. They freely exercised the ballot and, out of gratitude to Abraham Lincoln, were Republicans. One candidate of Lincoln's party, however, lost his election for a courthouse office when he quipped to a white rally that he had just come from "blackberrying" for votes. More seasoned politicians carefully tended their fences in the East End.

In this environment I spent my youth. I accepted as a matter of course the diversified make-up of the American people, for it formed part of my daily experience. It always puzzled me that the school histories should give the United States only one mother country when it possessed so many. This attitude proved all the more natural since I myself was on both sides of immigrant parentage.

My mother, Katharine Feurle, born in the Austrian village of Kennelbach in the German Tyrol, came with her Catholic parents, John George and Rosina Feurle, to Xenia in 1853 at the age of three. There her father—my grandfather—kept a lodging and boarding house which catered to his German compatriots. Though he died a decade or so before my birth, my grandmother continued to occupy the sprawling frame building with some of her children and grandchildren. How she made ends meet I do not know, for she had given up the tavern business. On rainy days the big, dimly lit attic held a particular charm for us young folk. In it, amid pieces of discarded furniture, were stacked great piles of unbound files of *Leslie's Illustrated Daily, Harper's Weekly,* and other Civil War journals which, to my grief in after years, we used as ammunition in our own pitched battles. And the grapevine-covered beer garden in the rear, now unused of course but retaining the old sturdy wooden tables and benches, made a fascinating playground in fair weather.

My father, Bernhard Schlesinger, was born in 1846 at Koenigswalde, a small town in East Prussia, the son of Nathan

Schlesinger, a horse dealer, and his wife, Marianne, both of the Jewish faith. In May, 1860, he emigrated to Newark, N.J., where, joining an older brother who had made a start in the leather business, he helped turn out knapsacks for the Union army during the Civil War. Then, seeking greener fields, he settled in Xenia in 1865, to remain there until his death in 1920. The land of promise subsequently drew across the Atlantic a younger brother and sister as well as a half-brother, all to different parts of the country but maintaining touch with the other members of the family. In Xenia, Father met petite Kate Feurle, and on February 20, 1873, they were married by the pastor of the German Reformed Church. To them in due course were born five children: my sisters, Olga and Marion, followed by my brothers, Hugo and George, and, finally, on February 27, 1888, by me. I probably was a surprise arrival.

Mother had two sisters, Rosina and Mathilda, both natives of Xenia, who also married Germans, and the young people of the three families totaled an even dozen of cousins. After the Old World fashion we shared a strong tribal feeling, preferring one another's company to that of other playmates. Holidays indeed were almost ritualistic affairs, each observed in a special fashion. On Christmas every household began the day to itself with the children emptying the stockings hung over the coal fireplace the night before, gaping at the decorated cedar tree rising grandly from floor to ceiling, then pouncing on the presents underneath; afterward we trudged to our cousins' homes laden with gifts for them. On New Year's Eve the clan assembled at Aunt Mathilda's for supper and an evening of song, climaxed by the shooting off of skyrockets at midnight. Where the pyrotechnic feature originated I do not know but always supposed it to have come from Germany. Before I was six I had learned to play the piano by ear, and on these occasions I presided at the keyboard, thumping as loud as I could to be heard above the voices. German folksongs were the rule with the latest American tunes interspersed. To my continuing regret I never learned to read music. Olga tried valiantly to teach me, but, as is still the case with so many youngsters, I proved rebellious. To this day I cannot read a note.

On the Fourth of July the kinsfolk congregated in the evening on our front lawn for a picnic supper of fried chicken, stewed oysters, and other toothsome viands, some furnished by the guests. The group was larger than on New Year's Eve, for outsiders were this time included. As dusk descended, the children set off all sorts of fireworks—flower pots, Roman candles, pinwheels, skyrockets, giant crackers, sparklers, and the rest—for which we had been saving our pennies. In addition, one of my cousins and I usually concocted a few exhibits of our own by mixing the ingredients of those we had bought. By good fortune we never lost life or limb. Many years later, in the Xenia *Herald*, June 24, 1943, the editor recalled these celebrations, which he had observed as a neighbor boy, and incidentally gave a picture of the house and its setting. "The Schlesinger home on S. Detroit St.," he wrote,

was a friendly, comfortable, rambling frame structure enriched by a good family life and the voices of children. It stood high from the street level and back from the street behind solid shade trees and a stone parapet that banked the terrace. . . . Independence Days were especially fine days, because there was a deep appreciation of the country and its generous opportunities in this family, and they liked to make the day a special occasion. There friends of the family gathered and, when the annual display of night fireworks was signaled by the approaching darkness, neighbors moved their chairs to their lawns so that they too could enjoy the exhibition.

Small boys were permitted to intrude, for there was none in this family to say them nay. Barefooted and grimy, powder-burned from a day of firing their own crackers and waking the dead with dynamite caps . . . , they gathered, fatigued, on the stone wall to await the big occasion of the evening. . . . And afterward, when there was ice cream for the Schlesingers and their guests, there were also saucers of ice cream for the grimy small boys who had been vigorously applauding on the stone wall so that their presence would not be ignored.

You just couldn't do anything on Hallowe'en night to people like that, could you? Woe to the lad who ever tried it.

Life in our household ran an even course despite the fact that Father never proved very successful at business. He had started out as a clerk in a clothing store, then became proprietor of a drygoods store. When I first remember him, he was a fire-insurance agent, which he continued to be till his death. Somehow he managed to support a wife and five young ones as well as to employ a nursemaid-housekeeper to assist Mother. Whatever his financial worries, we never lacked for ordinary comforts or ever felt envious of children who had more prosperous parents. We boys earned spending money by delivering papers, depositing some of the proceeds in the Xenia Building and Loan Association against emergencies. My own little nest egg, though necessarily drawn upon from time to time, remained there accumulating interest until some years after my marriage.

Father, a stout, mustached, reticent man afflicted with a hernia which obliged him to walk with a cane, was the final arbiter in family arguments, seldom speaking otherwise. Like so many German-Americans, he had an ardent interest in public education, all the keener perhaps because he himself had stopped short of the Prussian equivalent of the American high school. From 1881 to 1919—nearly forty years—he served on the Xenia School Board, a body chosen by popular vote, usually as its meagerly paid secretary. This indicates something of the esteem he enjoyed in the community. Mother, small of frame and quick in movement, is a dimmer figure. She was a chronic worrier over trifles and lacked Father's intellectual bent. She spent hours with her head bowed over fancywork. Though taking obvious pride in her children, she did not find it easy to express affection and never to my knowledge exerted a telling influence on any of us. It may be that because I was the youngest I in particular did not feel close to her, being more apt to confide my hopes and cares to Lizzie Bowser, our housekeeper.

A daughter of German-born parents, Lizzie had come from the nearby hamlet of Old Town as an eleven-year-old girl to help out when Olga was born and had made herself so indispensable that she remained with us until both my parents died and the Detroit Street home was broken up in 1927. Although she had little formal education, she possessed high native intelligence and a warmly sympathetic nature. She thought of herself as a member of the family and so did we. She always ate at the table with us and later joined us in the living room. And all our friends regarded her in the same light. As a matter of course, when her time came, she was laid to rest in the family lot in the town cemetery.

My boyhood could hardly have been pleasanter. Xenia lay within easy walking distance of a large woods and several streams. In the spring I plucked wild flowers, transplanting the choicer species to our yard, a habit I still follow, though now with regrettably less zeal. In the summer we would go fishing or gather at favorite swimming holes, and sometimes the kinsfolk would rent a picnic wagon for a day's outing at some interesting scenic spot. When autumn came the diversion was nutting, with a sideline of knocking down persimmons, which then had to be sweetened in the sun before eating. And winter brought coasting, along with gay parties for long bobsleigh rides in the moonlight. Fishing deserves a further word, even though our homemade poles and bent pins seldom caught anything bigger than minnows. That the fault lay with us was spectacularly demonstrated when a distillery at Trebein, a crossroads village on the Miami River a few miles away, burst into flames one night in August, 1904. The firemen, in order to save the whole structure from burning, diverted the raw alcohol into the stream, intoxicating the fish and causing them to wallow about helplessly on the surface. The next morning it seemed as if all Xenia were on hand with baskets and buckets to scoop them up. This is one fish story I can vouch for.

There were also distractions of a different sort. We listened with utter fascination to patent-medicine men who, arrayed in Indian garb and spitting tobacco juice, held forth after dark under flickering kerosene torches in their wagons before the courthouse. Strumming banjoes and singing hilarious ditties to attract a crowd, they would then vaunt their miraculous concoctions for the tapeworm, consumption, and other alarming ailments. From time to time one-ring circuses and dog-and-pony shows also came to Xenia, and on one unforgettable occasion in the summer of 1902 or 1903 Buffalo Bill's Wild West Show. In anticipation the whole county grew excited, and to cash in on the expected attendance the townsfolk set up along the sidewalks booths heaped with sandwiches and tubs of lemonade. Well, the great day arrived with its exhibitions of sharpshooting, frontiersmen in covered wagons beating off redskins, and other astounding feats; but the weatherman had neglected to co-operate, and a deluge of rain reduced the out-of-town patrons almost to zero. That night sandwiches were a drug on the market. My father, like many another thrifty parent, loaded up with a big supply, and for days afterward the family ate them as the buns grew harder and the butter more rancid. But we youngsters did not think this too big a sacrifice for the marvels we had seen.

In my high-school days I served as an unpaid usher in the opera house. Xenia was too small to attract many good shows, but I witnessed an unending succession of slapstick farces and blood-and-thunder melodramas. *Uncle Tom's Cabin,* a hardy perennial, drew capacity audiences even when, as a *Gazette* reviewer put it, the bloodhounds were poorly supported. This experience apparently wrought no harm. On the contrary, it whetted my appetite for better stage fare, so that, when my pocketbook permitted, I rode the sixteen miles by interurban trolley to Dayton and from the topmost gallery of the Victoria Theater viewed well-acted musical comedies and serious plays. In that way I first saw such stars of New York fame as George M. Cohan, Raymond Hitchcock, and Julia Marlowe. By this time, too, I had begun to go to dances. In the winter they were held in the Knights of Pythias hall, the only sizable floor in town. In the summer we went by a swaying trolley to Neff Park, nine miles away, where the pavilion, set amid oaks and elms, looked romantically down on a small, rippling lake. The music, to our complete satisfaction, consisted of a drum and piano played by a young Negro and his sister, to which we danced slow-rhythmed waltzes and two-steps.

Of the religious side of life I was largely an onlooker. As a small boy, however, I regularly attended the Sunday school of the German Reformed sect, where my cousins also went, but neither then nor in after years did I join that or any other church. Our Sabbath teacher, the pastor's wife, would relate simple Scriptural stories without any attempt to enlarge on them or to separate myth from historical fact; but, on the other hand, she never sought to frighten us with the terrors of hell-fire. My mother, though herself no churchgoer, felt that in a community so strongly devout her children should do as their playmates did, while Father, who, as I came to know later, was an agnostic, maintained a hands-off attitude.

Nearly every Christian denomination had a devoted following. One of the strictest, the United Presbyterians, conducted a local theological seminary. As special events, traveling Methodist evangelists now and then showed up, creating a furor among young and old in and outside their fold. I attended a few of the meetings at the urging of companions; and while the praying and exhorting deeply stirred my emotions—had not I, too, at times lied and committed other transgressions? —I resented the climactic plea to all true believers to rise to their feet and evidence publicly their commitment to Christ.

This seemed an unwarranted invasion of personal privacy, and I remained obstinately if uneasily in my seat. For the revival's duration the Methodist young people would abandon dancing and cards, but when things returned to normal again, so would they. This did nothing to instill in me a regard for outward professions of piety.

From as far back as I can remember I was a voracious reader. The three or four hundred volumes in our own bookcase outnumbered those of any other family of our acquaintance and included, along with German works and a set of Shakespeare of Father's, the standard New England poets and the complete writings of Thackeray, George Eliot, and Washington Irving, which Olga had obtained. In addition, I made use of the public library, which maintained a well-chosen collection. The librarian, Miss Etta G. McElwain, prim, sparrow-like, and brusque, with sharp eyes behind shining spectacles, had little patience with children who resorted there simply to idle away time, but she was an invaluable counselor and friend to those who loved her treasures.

When I reached the age of fourteen I listed the books which I could recall as having read, 598 in all. Heading the authors were G. A. Henty (49 titles), Kirk Munro (27), and W. G. Stoddard (20), followed by "James Otis" (J. O. Kaler) (16), Mark Twain (12), Horatio Alger (8), James Fenimore Cooper (5), and Louisa May Alcott (5). Of a more mature character were the volumes by Frank R. Stockton (16), A. Conan Doyle (10), Stanley J. Weyman (9), Robert Louis Stevenson (8), Anthony Hope (7), Paul Du Chaillu (6), Alexandre Dumas (6), and F. Marion Crawford (5). Among still others were Daniel Defoe's *Robinson Crusoe,* Harriet Beecher Stowe's *Uncle Tom's Cabin,* Edward Bellamy's *Looking Backward,* Cervantes' *Don Quixote,* Jonathan Swift's *Gulliver's Travels,* Mary Mapes Dodge's *Hans Brinker,* and one or more by Hawthorne, Irving, Scott, Dickens, Howells, Henry James, Richard Harding Davis, H. Rider Haggard,

Gilbert Parker, James Barrie, H. G. Wells, Bret Harte, Lew Wallace, F. Hopkinson Smith, George W. Cable, Owen Wister, Winston Churchill (the American), Ellen Glasgow, Robert W. Chambers, and Hamlin Garland.

Even aside from the authors left unmentioned, this constituted a decidedly varied diet and in part an indigestible one for a youngster. Some of the books I did not properly appreciate until I reread them in more mature years. The majority, however, were rousing adventure stories made more real by the inclusion of historical characters and episodes. In particular, as is apparent, I fell captive to G. A. Henty. A British journalist who had reported on the spot the Crimean War, he had turned to penning fictional accounts of past days ranging all the way from ancient Egypt to the trans-Mississippi American frontier, with a boy always as the central character. Henty was still writing when I was growing up, and each new book was a red-letter event in my eyes. Only in two instances did my loyalty falter. These books were *True to the Old Flag* and *With Lee in Virginia,* tales of the Revolutionary and Civil wars, where Henty's English viewpoint led him to make a Tory youth the hero of the one and a Southern lad of the other. I secured as many of his volumes as I could for my personal library, and years later my sons read them with equal enjoyment. A man seldom knows just what causes him to choose his life career, but I do not doubt that in my case this love of Henty was one formative influence.

In school I was a conscientious pupil and was blessed with good teachers from the elementary grades through the high school. This was in the days before educational "frills." We were expected to work hard and most of us did. My high-school course (1902-06) consisted of four years of English and of history, four of Latin (from Caesar to Vergil), four of mathematics (through solid geometry), two of German and two of science (treating the elements of botany, physiology, physics, and chemistry). Of the teaching staff Miss Anna Mc-

Cracken in Latin made the most lasting impression. A plump fuss-budget of a woman with a squeaky voice, she was a wretched disciplinarian, but she imparted the essentials of the language in a way serious students were not likely soon to forget. One device was to require beginners to memorize the entire first chapter of Caesar, since it contained all the grammatical constructions they would come across later. To this day I can repeat the first third of that chapter. Her unusual intellectual background is suggested by the fact that she was the sister of the president of New York University and the aunt of Vassar's president.

Graduating at the head of my class, it fell to me to deliver the valedictory address at commencement. The exercises were held, according to custom, in the opera house, with each member making a speech of his own. Though we started off at nine in the morning, my turn did not come till early in the afternoon without any break for lunch. My discourse, somewhat flowerily entitled "The Approach of the Dawn," was an attack on unrestricted economic competition and a plea for the government ownership of the railroads and other public utilities. The year was 1906, Teddy Roosevelt reigned in the White House, political progressivism was on the march, so such ideas were very much in the air. Actually, however, I had been more directly influenced by Bellamy's vision of the year 2000 in *Looking Backward*.

Though Xenia was in most respects a self-contained world, various things, some out of the past, served to remind the people that they shared as well in the life of the nation. Not the least was the presence of Civil War veterans, wizened ancients, many with wooden legs. The G.A.R., its membership steadily dwindling, commanded universal awe and incidentally helped tighten the hold of the Republican party on the community. Each year on Decoration Day—it was not yet called Memorial Day—a procession to the cemetery laid wreaths on the graves of the heroic dead, with the children of the town looking solemnly on. In addition there was a Sons of Veterans band which performed on public occasions. More intimately, pictures of the days of valor adorned nearly every home. In my parents' bedroom, for instance, hung a chromo of a soldier astride a mule, entitled "Going Home on a Furlough." The scene fired my childish imagination, and it was only long afterward that I found out somewhat incredulously that a furlough was not an animal. My father, as has already been noted, had himself taken no part in the fighting. He had come to America when he was thirteen, about a year before the conflict began, and did not reach draft age till its close.

Apart from these reminders of dead-and-gone times, my first clear recollection of happenings outside Xenia relates to the World's Columbian Exposition at Chicago in 1893 when I was five. Mother and Father attended and brought back prized souvenirs, but my sharper remembrance arises from seeing a strange glow in the skies one night which my playmates and I promptly attributed to the fair's reflected lights. It was in vain for our elders to tell us that it was the aurora borealis. Certain other youthful memories also abide. One is of the Bryan campaign of 1896 when the "Boy Orator of the Platte" briefly invaded our Republican fastness, speaking from the rear platform of a train. As one of the little band present, I shook his hand; in fact, in my excitement I did so twice. A further memory is of an uncle who a year later joined the gold rush to the Klondike and returned broke but full of his adventures. Another is of the Spanish-American War, reflected locally in intense anger at the sinking of the *Maine* and then jubilation over Dewey's victory at Manila. Still another is of a trip in 1901 to the Pan-American Exposition in Buffalo with Lizzie and a boy companion. Finally, there was the shooting of President McKinley on the Exposition grounds a few months afterward. I was at a lawn party when the news came, and we were all so unbelieving that we laughed to one another that he must have been shot with a camera.

In Xenia itself the ever-recurrent political issue was prohibition, which on election day sometimes went one way and sometimes the other. Father and other Germans, accustomed to beer and wine in their homes, felt bitterly on the subject, scoring temperance advocates as sheer bigots. Indeed, drunkards were a rare sight on the streets and seldom proved troublesome. Yet, had a like ban been proposed on cigarettes, he would undoubtedly have been one of the first to favor it. For reasons which I have never been able to fathom, that would not have seemed to him to violate the principle of "personal liberty" which he so firmly avowed in the case of alcoholic beverages. It was only young men in those years—never women—who had the addiction, and to many of the older generation cigarettes were "coffin nails" or at any rate evidence of a loose character. (Recent medical findings as to their effect in inducing lung cancer lend belated authority to the disease-promoting thesis.) Father, ordinarily a courteous man, would not even give a match to a cigarette smoker, and he instilled in me a youthful bias that has ever since deterred me from acquiring the habit. He himself enjoyed cigars and, as I grew up, he encouraged me also to do so or to smoke a pipe.

In national affairs he was a sturdy Democrat of the Cleveland stripe. Inasmuch as the New Yorker was President when I entered the world, he even wished to name me Grover instead of Arthur; but my sisters vetoed it. The rise of Bryanism excited his misgivings, though not to the extent of deserting the party. To the very end his political outlook remained largely an almost religious belief in the virtues of a low tariff. He could hardly have done otherwise than disapprove of the tone of my commencement address, but, characteristically, he did not say so. Those were matters which by his canons a son of his must decide for himself, though I feel certain he hoped that in the three years before attaining voting age I would arrive at more sensible views.

II

Going to College

It was taken for granted by both the family and me that I should attend the Ohio State University. That conformed with the plan Olga had originated after she, the first of the children, had been denied a higher education by Father's lack of means. This misfortune, she resolved, should not befall the rest of us. Accordingly, from her pay as a sixth-grade teacher she helped Marion go through the German-American Teachers Seminary in Milwaukee. Then Marion, upon becoming a German instructor at a high school near Xenia, chipped in to send Hugo through Ohio State in Columbus, including the Law School; and in turn the three did the same for George, whose choice was civil engineering. As I was ready to enter a year before George finished, I had either to hold off for the time or enroll on my own. I decided not to wait, since I could draw on my earnings during the preceding four years as local agent of the Cincinnati *Times-Star*. After the Freshman year, of course, I received the customary family assistance.

Inasmuch as Hugo and George had preceded me, I had some notion of what to expect. Beginning a new life away from home was therefore not the challenge it might otherwise have proved, and in any event the University was but two hours by train from Xenia. During the first year, moreover, George remained on the ground, though he was too busy with his engineering classes to see very much of me. Almost at once I joined Phi Delta Theta, their fraternity, but reasons of economy led me to room and eat elsewhere, and this enabled me quickly to enlarge the circle of my friends. The students as a matter of course came mostly from Ohio, though there was a generous sprinkling from other states and a scattering from foreign countries as well. After the Freshman year Hugo and his wife, Mary, moved to Columbus near the campus. He had found Xenia too limited a field for the practice of law. During the remainder of the time, I lived with them, and things could not have turned out better. Hugo, ten years my senior, had an active and inquiring mind and proved a constant spur to my own intellectual endeavors, while his attractive helpmate, a former domestic-science teacher, set a table which rivaled if it did not surpass Lizzie's at home. Eventually he was elected prosecuting attorney of the county—an indication of the place he made for himself in the larger community.

The years at Ohio State from 1906 to 1910 deepened my mental perceptions, brought new associations and interests, determined my choice of a life career, and, for good measure, introduced me to the young lady who was to be my wife. If I possessed any clear-cut aim at the outset, it was to become a newspaperman. This no doubt sprang from already having had some amateur experience. As a high-school Senior I had written up student happenings for the Xenia *Gazette* and at various times had replaced the local correspondent of a Springfield daily when he was on vacation. Perhaps, too, Richard Harding Davis's absorbing reports of the Spanish-American and Boer wars had made journalism seem a glamorous calling. The University, however, provided no instruction in the subject, so I had no alternative but to choose from among the regular offerings of the College of Arts, Philosophy and Science.

For the Freshman and Sophomore years the faculty permitted a fairly free selection; accordingly I signed up for English, German, Latin and French, geology and chemistry, psychology, history, political science, economics, and sociology. No courses were then available in anthropology, to my continued later regret. In addition, the University as a land-grant institution obliged the men throughout two years to take military training. Every morning at eleven, weather permitting, we drilled for an hour in blue uniforms mostly of second-hand origin, shouldering antique bulletless Springfield rifles, while on frigid or stormy days we pored over a manual of tactics dating from the Civil War era. By and large we made glum soldiers. In fact, the whole business held little meaning for us. The world had witnessed no major conflict since the Franco-Prussian War of 1870-71, and the Permanent Court of International Arbitration, set up at The Hague in 1899, obviously signified the wave of the future. Moreover, the demand for unquestioning obedience contrasted starkly with the independent thinking expected in the classroom. But to flunk the requirement meant to repeat the ordeal, and that sufficed to make me into a model cadet. Incidentally, James Thurber, a more rebellious soul, who arrived on the scene a half-dozen or so years afterward, had to keep on drilling even when a Senior. In his case, however, it provided him in later life with material for one of the funniest sketches of his youthful days.

In the upper two years, marked by greater specialization, I bore down heavily on advanced work in United States history, with political science as my minor subject. This brought me in close classroom association with three members of the faculty whose teaching and example cured me for all time of the half-formed idea of entering journalism. George Wells Knight, head of the Department of American History, was a pale, smallish, low-waisted man with thinning gray hair who had the gift of dissecting a complex historical issue with relentless logic, reducing it to polar terms of black and white. One felt that his was the only possible view, that only the stupid or the malevolent at the time of the event could ever have thought differently. To his students Knight seemed a peerless teacher, an opinion which he gave evidence of sharing himself. It was not until I reached Graduate School that I came to realize that human situations seldom lend themselves to such categorical treatment; that the analysis of a historical problem may well yield multiple answers; indeed, that this is the normal characteristic of the historical process. Henry Russell Spencer, head of the Political Science Department, possessed, as I dimly perceived even then, a more sophisticated intelligence. Stocky in build with a swarthy complexion and an abrupt manner of speech, he sometimes talked over the heads of his students, but he stretched the minds of the better ones as did few other professors under whom I sat.

The third of the trio, Clarence A. Dykstra, a handsome young instructor whose Byronic profile caused heart flutterings among the girls, taught both political science and American history. By sheer gusto he furthered my interest in history, lending it an air of continuous excitement. But "Dyke," to my regret, departed at the end of my Junior year to accept a better position at the University of Kansas. By letter and occasional meetings, however, we continued to keep in touch. After some years he abandoned the classroom to serve with distinction in such varied capacities, among others, as city manager of Cincinnati, president of the University of Wisconsin, and, finally, provost of the University of California at Los Angeles. A few weeks before his death in 1950, when I stayed the night with him in Los Angeles, he said he still had in his files a course report I had written for him on the disintegration of the Federalist party.

United States history was in those days at Ohio State political history, a record of constitutional development, party strife, diplomacy and wars, with only cursory attention to economic aspects and none at all to such influences as education, literature, and the role of the foreign-born. Religious factors received no mention after the colonial period, and humanitarian movements only in the unavoidable connection with the antislavery cause. In Freeman's aphorism, history was past politics, politics present history. Homer C. Hockett, who had been secretary to Frederick Jackson Turner while working for his doctorate at Wisconsin, came as an associate professor in my Senior year and offered for the first time there a course on The Westward Movement; but I neglected to take it. In any event, the Turner school, too, was primarily concerned with the political consequences of the expanding frontier.

The introductory course, which ended with the completion of Southern Reconstruction in 1877, before any of us were born, was conducted by means of recitation and discussion based on *Epochs of American History,* a set of three pocket-size volumes written respectively by Reuben Gold Thwaites, Albert Bushnell Hart, and Woodrow Wilson, then president of Princeton. In the advanced classes the professors delivered lectures, required term papers (like the one for Dykstra), and prescribed considerable collateral reading. The most frequent assignments were to the *American Statesman* series, edited in the 1880's by John T. Morse, Jr., and to the yet uncompleted *American Nation* series which, under Hart's direction, presented the findings of the latest scholarship. In addition, we used the multivolume histories of James Ford Rhodes and John Bach McMaster, both of which were also still being published, as well as older works. The University Library contained all that was needed for undergraduates, also some key collections of printed sources, though I do not recall we were ever referred to these. Probably this was because our instructors, though well read in their subjects, were not themselves research men.

A year after graduation I summed up my over-all reactions to my college education in a letter to Elizabeth Bancroft (of whom more later). The judgments were probably hyper-

critical, at least in view of the way most American institutions
of higher learning were conducted at the time. The last two
years, I wrote, had hardly been worth while, since they had
done little more than to amplify without importantly adding
to what had earlier been learned. In addition,

The teaching throughout was unsuccessful in stimulating interest in
subject matter related to but not included in the actual courses.
That is, a student reads Shakespeare and Browning in his English
courses but leaves without any curiosity as to who such of his own
contemporaries as Chesterton and Arnold Bennett are. Or he takes
work in political science and doesn't know—or care—how his city
is governed or who the chairman of the ways and means committee
of Congress is. It is really lamentable.

This test of instruction as an incentive to matters which should
stem naturally from the knowledge gained would be an interesting one to apply to colleges today.

   In extracurricular activities one could be about as busy as
he wished. I had no aptitude for dramatics or the glee club
or sports—except as a zealous rooter—but, finding myself
when a Sophomore with some free time, I began to gather
items for the *Lantern,* the undergraduate weekly, and became
one of the two assistant editors the next year. This put me on
the ladder for editor in chief in my Senior year, provided I
could turn in more inches of copy than the other assistant editor. The position, moreover, meant sharing with the business
manager the profits of the paper. In this competition I
enjoyed an initial advantage by being asked to report the
weekly chapel talks of the president of the University, and
these write-ups probably did more than anything else to enable me to achieve the promotion.

   The chapel assignment fortunately proved no irksome one,
since William Oxley Thompson, though an ordained Presbyterian minister, avoided sectarian narrowness, stressing instead
ethical principles and illustrating them with many an appeal-
ing homely instance. His craggy features and thickset figure

reminded me irresistibly of pictures of Daniel Webster. Attendance by students had not for many years been compulsory, but nonetheless they generally filled the hall, partly no doubt because it was their only opportunity to come in contact with his kindly personality before their graduation exercises. President Thompson, as I came to realize more fully after I joined the teaching staff, was in no sense an educational statesman, but he usually proved able to keep peace in the faculty and to secure most of the funds requested of the legislature.

In my position of editor in chief I spent nearly as much of my final year on the *Lantern* as on my classes. The paper consisted of four pages of ordinary newspaper size devoted exclusively to campus affairs, with special departments given over to athletics and social events plus a column of Addisonian comment on the beauties of nature and like topics by a popular English professor. The only marked change from previous years was a weekly cartoon by a classmate, Ray O. Evans, who later served in a similar capacity successively on the Baltimore *News and American* and the Columbus *Dispatch*. Ray too, however, confined himself to college happenings. Otherwise we endeavored to provide a more systematic coverage of student and faculty doings than had been customary. I wrote all the editorials, revised stories assigned to reporters, and put together a regular column of news of other universities. At the printing office in downtown Columbus the key members of the staff worked every Monday evening till midnight to make up the sheet and put it to bed. I learned more about writing from this practical experience than from all my English courses combined.

When the time came in the spring of my Senior year to nominate a successor, I recommended as a matter of course the assistant editor who had handed in the lion's share of copy. This, however, precipitated a violent row with the student board of control—made up of fraternity men—because he was not a "brother" whereas the losing candidate was. I probably should have anticipated the difficulty, for membership in Phi Delta Theta had made me aware of the extent to which the Greek-letter societies strove to monopolize every important undergraduate office. On the one hand, they competed fiercely among themselves for all campus distinctions; on the other, they formed a united front to shut out the "barbarians," who made up the mass of the student body. Even so, I had not believed that the board of control would cynically ignore the plain letter of the by-laws. Yet this is precisely what they did. My opposition proved vain, and in the end I had to appeal to a faculty body to correct the flagrant injustice.

As this indicates, I myself was not in the accepted sense a good fraternity man. I knew and enjoyed too many interesting and worth-while fellows beyond the pale. The one undeniable justification for the clans was that they afforded their members pleasant living and dining quarters. The University at that time maintained no dormitories, thus leaving most undergraduates to fend for themselves as best they could in the private houses fringing the campus. This boon for the few, however, was largely negated by the fact that the fraternities typically valued athletic over intellectual prowess and inevitably tended to social snobbery. A still greater fault, though then I was unaware of it, was that the national constitutions of most if not all the groups denied admission to nonwhites and Jews—this in a country historically committed to democratic ideals. The reason no doubt for my ignorance was that there were so few colored and Jewish students at the University that the question never actually arose as regards my own fraternity. It was not until long, long afterward, in fact not till 1954, that the restrictive clause first came to my knowledge through an item in the press. The piece related that a general convention of Phi Delta Theta, after opening its proceedings with singing "The Star-Spangled Banner," had, over the protests of undergraduate delegates, stoutly reaffirmed the ban, though now in more tactful language. Incidentally, this was the very year of the Supreme Court's famous school-desegregation decision. Since as an alumnus I was still nominally a member, I wrote a letter to the national president berating the persisting bigotry and submitted my resignation. After some weeks he replied that the rules did not permit me to resign; I could only be expelled. So, to our mutual gratification, I returned to the ranks of the unanointed nearly half a century after my initiation.

Toward the end of my Junior year I was chosen to membership in the Sphinx Society. Eligibility to this small self-perpetuating body of Seniors depended on prominence in extracurricular activities, and I no doubt qualified as prospective editor in chief of the *Lantern*. On Link Day, as the occasion was called, the students, spread over the sward in front of University Hall at the appointed time, watched and waited while the black-robed brethren weaved in and out and linked arms with their successors. This was the highest possible accolade in student eyes. Toward the close of my final year I was further named with a dozen others to Phi Beta Kappa, a lesser honor in undergraduate opinion inasmuch as the selection rested on scholastic marks. In retrospect I have often wondered what predictive value either type of achievement at this stage of life has as to future promise, since, to my knowledge, none of my fellows in either group with a single exception later attained comparable recognition.

Downtown Columbus lay a mile from the campus. To reach it meant either a time-consuming tramp over hard sidewalks through a dreary part of the city or a bumpy ride on the trolley with stops at nearly every corner. The two worlds therefore had little contact. About the only attractions for students were the theater and, for the religious-minded, some outstanding preacher. Above all, Keith's Vaudeville House proved a magnet because of the low admission charge. One night, to the great glee of my companions, a comedian unexpectedly burst out:

Tell me, oh tell me please,
Is Xenia a town or a disease?

This couplet was dinned into my ears for weeks thereafter. I also saw occasional musical comedies, arriving early to line up for the cheapest seats. I remember in particular a Negro troupe which featured Bert Williams, who was later to star with white entertainers in the *Ziegfeld Follies* and other Broadway shows. Of serious plays, Maude Adams in *What Every Woman Knows* and David Warfield in *The Music Master* stand out.

With less regularity I attended the First Congregational Church on East Broad Street, drawn by the pastor's benign character. Dr. Washington Gladden, though no longer the dynamic civic reformer of earlier days, was still a nationally influential exponent of the social gospel. His quietly delivered sermons appealed to the mind as well as to the heart. In his message of "Applied Christianity"—the title of one of his best-known books—he communicated a moving sense of the power of human goodness in personal and community life. With his great, flowing white beard and noble forehead he looked not unlike Michelangelo's conception of God.

Absorbed as most students were in day-to-day concerns, they displayed slight interest in the nation's affairs notwithstanding that Theodore Roosevelt while he held office took pains to expound as few Presidents have the crying issues of the day. The closest approach to an undergraduate political club was the local chapter of the Intercollegiate Socialist Society, which I sometimes attended, but its few members concentrated on Marxian theory with little or no reference to practical action. A Political Science Club also existed under the wing of Professors Knight and Spencer, and I was president of it one year; but it was content to discuss papers, usually warmed-over class reports, on subjects which at best had remote current application.

Even the presidential contest of 1908, falling in my Junior year, created little stir. For me, however, it afforded my first view of William Jennings Bryan, now running for a third time, since I had shaken his hand—twice—as an eight-year-old in Xenia; and it also gave me my very first sight of the dynamic Teddy. Both held forth in downtown halls, Roosevelt to laud Secretary of War Taft as his hand-picked successor. No two public figures could have offered a greater contrast. I listened enthralled to the rich, organlike tones of Bryan, whom I still consider the most eloquent, though hardly the profoundest, political orator I have ever heard. By comparison, Roosevelt spoke in a rasping voice, which often rose to the falsetto, and seemed to rely for rhetorical effect on arm-pumping gesticulations and his famous toothy smile. From the strictly Ohio standpoint, though, these headliners were eclipsed by the address of William Randolph Hearst. Early in the campaign the widely known yellow journalist, ambitious for political power, had founded what proved to be the short-lived Independence party; and to expose the malpractices of the administration in office he seized the occasion to air a batch of letters from John D. Archbold of the Standard Oil Company to Senator Joseph B. Foraker, which showed that the veteran Buckeye Republican stalwart, now seeking re-election, had taken pay of nearly $30,000 from the giant monopoly. All this he divulged in an almost listless manner as if his words required no dramatic emphasis. Taft, of course, swept the country, including his native Ohio, while Foraker, unable to explain the unexplainable, was retired permanently to private life.

My two closest friends in college were Thomas Hoyt Jones and James Cooper Lawrence. Both were serious-minded students without being bookworms. Tom, a fraternity mate, achieved the unusual distinction of being simultaneously captain of the football team and a member of Phi Beta Kappa— almost a mixing of oil and water. A native of Jackson, Ohio, he was the son of a judge of the state supreme court and was himself headed for the law. We took many of the same courses and in summers visited in each other's homes. He was one of the few I knew, except for the handful of avowed Socialists, who gave any thought to the country's economic and social problems. Once he went so far as to advocate a 100-per-cent inheritance tax as the best way to redistribute wealth and ensure equality of opportunity; and this was before the provision even for an income tax had been put into the Constitution. But after finishing the Law School he joined a firm of corporation attorneys in Cleveland, and his views underwent a profound change. When I ran across him sometime around 1935—I was then at Harvard—he denounced my colleague and friend Felix Frankfurter as the evil architect of the New Deal and "the most dangerous man in America." That was the last time I ever saw him, for he died prematurely not long afterward.

Jimmie Lawrence lacked the personal qualities that made Tom Jones universally liked and respected, but he had a quick intelligence and a buoyant and obliging nature, and we, too, possessed many interests in common. The son of a Columbus physician, he lived in a somewhat eccentric household, where I was always warmly welcome. To many of his contemporaries he seemed too effusive, if not overaggressive, and this probably kept him from ever making a fraternity, a circumstance which deeply wounded him and may have caused me to see more of him than otherwise. Upon becoming editor of the *Lantern* I had him conduct the sports page, and, besides performing that task expertly, he constantly sparked ideas for improving the rest of the paper. He expected to go into college teaching, but an abrupt change of plans following graduation sent him instead to the Goodrich Rubber Company in Akron. Meeting with success in that and later in other enterprises, he decided after twenty-odd years to realize his original ambition of entering academic life, though, in view of the loss of time, in an executive position. He became administrative aide to the president of the University of Minnesota and seemed well launched on his new career when, apparently because of financial difficulties, he committed suicide. Perhaps a psychiatrist could explain this gifted human being. I cannot.

But neither of these companions meant as much to my future well-being and happiness as a coed I met early in my Junior year. Elizabeth Bancroft was a Columbus girl, the daughter of a widowed mother who was employed in the local branch of the Federal Pension Bureau. A member of the Pi Beta Phi sorority, she had left college two years before, at the end of her Sophomore year, to teach in a one-room country school nearby to earn money with which to complete her work for the A.B. Of medium height and slender build with dark hair, fair skin, and chestnut-brown eyes, she attracted me equally by her alert mind and zest for life. Soon I began taking strolls with her between classes and to escort her to dances and other campus affairs. I was not, however, the only man she went around with—she had many admirers—nor was she the only girl I beaued; but as the weeks passed, we saw more and more of each other, and upon taking over the *Lantern* I seized the opportunity to have her close by as society editor.

We did not become formally engaged before graduation, but entertained no doubt as to our mutual feelings and what we hoped lay ahead for us. Before acting on that knowledge, however, we felt I should first be able to earn a living—today, to be sure, an archaic idea. My decision to prepare for an academic career resulted from the intellectual challenge of American history and the backing of my major professors, furthered by Hugo's encouragement and the unstinted approval of Elizabeth. I applied to Harvard as well as to Columbia for a tuition scholarship, hardly expecting either but obtaining both. It was largely due to Professor Spencer, a Columbia Ph.D in history, that I chose in the end to go where he himself had studied. With this award, plus my earnings as *Lantern* editor,

I could now count on at least one year of professional training. Elizabeth meanwhile secured a position as a high-school teacher of history in Kalamazoo, Michigan.

The commencement exercises in June occurred in a beautiful campus setting, with 401 men and girls obtaining their degrees and the beloved Washington Gladden delivering the address. While sitting with solemn thoughts at the ceremony, I noticed that the program listed one of my classmates as Grover Cleveland Portz, and I reflected that, but for the timely intervention of my sisters, I would have shared his lot.

That summer I spent with my parents in Xenia, helping Father with his insurance business, reading whatever came to hand, and wondering what the year to come held for me.

III

The Apprenticeship to History

What turned out to be two years at Columbia—1910 to 1912
—constituted an unforgettable experience. It proved a mental
shaking up comparable to what one would today call a break-
through. I not only exchanged physical surroundings but also
teachers, and both vitally advanced my intellectual development and social understanding. Though Columbus was a
town of fair size for the Middle West, I now lived on the Eastern seaboard in the country's foremost metropolis, a city out
of a storybook to an untraveled son of the Buckeye state. As
I was to say later in my volume of the *History of American
Life*, "Nowhere else in the nation were there such fine buildings, such imposing financial houses, such unusual opportunities for business and recreation. No other place offered such a
picture of rush and bustle, the streets constantly being torn
up, dug up or blown up." The air itself was exhilarating, im-
pelling one to be up and doing. Although, as an English visitor wrote, New York was like "a lady in ball costume, with
diamonds in her ears, and her toes out of her boots," that, too,
added to the fascination, for I had never before observed
such gross inequalities of living, the mansions of the unbeliev-

ably rich lording it over the incredible squalor of the poor. But even this aspect, grieving as it was to the human spirit, gave new meaning to the infinite variety—the disappointments as well as the successes—of the land of promise. Notwithstanding that my duties kept me more or less to Morningside Heights, nearly four miles away from Times Square, the heart of the city, I never lost the sense of being a part of this great pulsing world or of its being a part of me.

The very appearance of Columbia, its chastely designed buildings cheek by jowl, unrelieved by trees or lawn, contrasted strikingly with the indiscriminate architecture and sylvan setting of Ohio State, conveying a workaday atmosphere appropriate to the larger community where it stood. I lodged on the ground floor in one of the cheapest rooms of Livingston Hall, a graduate dormitory fronting on a flagged court off 116th Street opposite the classic-domed University Library. A large lounge with easy chairs and settees faced the entrance, and from it a dark corridor led off to my cubbyhole. Narrow and long, with its single window looking out on noisy Amsterdam Avenue, it was just large enough to accommodate one straight-backed chair, a study table with a bookrack, a chest of drawers, a couch-bed, a shallow clothes closet, and a washbowl with running water. Practically everything lay within arm's reach, being wholly sufficient for my simple requirements.

To reduce other expenses I prepared my breakfasts and lunches in a small aluminum bowl over an alcohol burner, probably in violation of the fire regulations; I never thought it prudent to inquire. The meals reflected my meager knowledge of cooking. A typical day's fare, I wrote Elizabeth Bancroft in Kalamazoo, consisted of an apple, shredded wheat with milk, and instant coffee in the morning, a cup of canned soup, potted-ham sandwiches, and another apple at noon. "This meets my needs," I observed, "and costs half as much as would eating out." At night I generally took advantage of a cut-rate meal ticket at the University Commons, where the food was ample though institutional in character. Fortunately I possessed three married cousins in Newark, N.J., daughters of the first Schlesinger to arrive in America, who welcomed me to their bountiful and appetizing tables whenever I was free. I would take the subway downtown to Fulton Street, then board a train crossing under the Hudson to Newark, the trip all told consuming about an hour and a half. I spent many Sundays as well as Thanksgivings and Christmases with them.

The work at Columbia opened windows and broke down walls. Having hitherto been taught by men who regurgitated the findings of others, I now sat at the feet of scholars who were themselves extending the bounds of knowledge. History, moreover, instead of being limited to government and politics, strove, with exceptions to be noted, to embrace all the agencies and conditions that had influenced man's development; and the professors in the sister social sciences reinforced the conception from their special angles. What a liberating force this proved, for as an undergraduate I had never understood why the study of history should rule out cultural and like potent factors in the life of society. If these affected, as they obviously did, the sentiments and actions of the individual, why did they not also those of individuals in the mass? In particular, American history and American literature, two subjects close to my heart, had been presented as though they did not have so much as a bowing acquaintance with each other.

James Harvey Robinson was the most articulate exponent of the "New History," the title of a widely discussed book which he brought out toward the end of my second year. His lectures on The History of the Intellectual Classes of Europe— from earliest to modern times—proved the most provocative of any I attended and triggered endless arguments among the students. So unsettling indeed were some of his ideas that we facetiously called the course "The Downfall of Christianity." Peering quizzically over his spectacles and impishly salting his observations with wit, he spoke quietly, as though interviewing himself with the class present merely as eavesdroppers. Robinson, it gradually dawned on me, was less interested in imparting his own thoughts than in exciting us to think for ourselves and to think, moreover, not only about the past but about the present state of mankind and what human intelligence, if properly directed, could do to better it.

Of Robinson's colleagues, Charles A. Beard in the Department of Politics made the deepest impression. Although Beard had not yet attained full rank, he had a large and enthusiastic student following. Fair-haired, vigorous in utterance, he endowed everything he said with a bracing air of realism, and his recurrent theme, as he later made evident in his writings, was the role of material self-interest in America's political and constitutional development. In no sense a Marxist or single-track economic determinist, he stressed—possibly over-stressed—an aspect which scholars had hitherto underplayed or ignored.

All this, however, is not to say that other professors did not afford their own stimulating insights into the past. A course with the sociologist Franklin H. Giddings, for example, amplified his concept of "consciousness of kind" as a vital key to social behavior, while the economist Edwin R. A. Seligman deepened my understanding of both economic history and economic theory. Of like value were two courses with Vladimir Simkhovich, of Seligman's department, which respectively treated the rise of international Socialism and nineteenth-century radical Russian literature, the latter involving wide reading of such writers as Turgenev, Kropotkin, and Kovalevsky and revealing the interplay of literature and politics in that then dimly known country. And to learn about the background of the non-Anglo-Saxon countries in the Western Hemisphere I attended William R. Shepherd's lectures on the evolution of Latin America. These men were more than just closet students. As government consultants or in other responsible capacities they had also acquired a practical grasp of their subjects, and in an undefinable way this lent greater authority to their words.

Oddly enough, the "New History" did not penetrate the confines of American history, where my principal interest lay, except as Beard dealt with the field. William A. Dunning and Herbert L. Osgood, the major professors, adhered to wholly traditional subject matter. Dunning, who handled the Civil War and Reconstruction periods, did so with an incisiveness to which his impeccable dress and white goatee somehow added a certain distinction; but he said little beyond what he had already written in his books. In fact he sometimes read directly from the proof sheets of one or another of them. Similarly, Professor Osgood viewed the colonial era from a legal and institutional angle. Having earlier brought out his path-breaking trilogy on the seventeenth century, he now was toiling day and night on what was to be his equally notable posthumous four-volume set on the pre-Revolutionary eighteenth century. Frail and somewhat bent, with domelike baldish head, he was a dry-as-dust lecturer who seldom raised his eyes from his laboriously handwritten manuscript. His course on the eighteenth century, reflecting his current researches, met on Saturday morning supposedly from eleven to one but hardly ever adjourned till well toward two. Like the little girl who said of a book on alligators that it told more about alligators than she wanted to know, I often felt he could have made his points more effectively with fewer details. Osgood, however, exemplified as no other of my professors the painstaking skills of historical inquiry and the self-discipline of disinterested judgment. He impressed himself on us as the very image of the austere and dedicated scholar, and for this I have never ceased to revere him.

With both men I elected seminars as well as lecture courses.

At Ohio State I had received little or no training in the spade-
work of history and indeed had formed the impression that
practically everything important was already known. In all
honesty my first seminar at Columbia, under Dunning on
Southern Reconstruction, did nothing to dispel the idea. The
research topics he assigned involved hardly more than a redo-
ing of what already had been done well enough. My own, on
the Congressional elections of 1866, had been competently
covered seven years before by David M. Dewitt in his excellent *Trial and Impeachment of Andrew Johnson.* Osgood's
seminar in the second year, however, proved a real eye-
opener, for he directed us to aspects of the eighteenth century
which had hitherto been neglected or misunderstood. My report on "Colonial Appeals to the Privy Council," for instance,
rested on recently issued documents of the British government; at his suggestion I later worked it over for the *Political
Science Quarterly.* But even in his lecture course Osgood had
the class write on subjects requiring original investigation. My
paper on "Maryland's Share in the Last Intercolonial War"
served as my Master's thesis and was published in the *Maryland Historical Magazine.* Neither effort, of course, made a far-
reaching contribution to scholarship, but the fact that I had
tried my wings and gotten off the ground provided welcome
confirmation of being in the right career.

Unfortunately, students, however desirous of closer contact
with their professors, had virtually no chance outside the
classroom. We never felt free to drop in at their offices, and
though they for the most part lived near the University, only
once was I invited to any of their homes—and then it was because Professor and Mrs. Osgood lacked young men at a
tea for their daughter Marian, home from Mt. Holyoke College for the Christmas vacation. A more informal association
would have made us feel less like passive consumers of their
learning and might even have yielded some benefit to them.
In that belief, when the time came for me to instruct graduate

students, I sought to establish a different and mutually profitable relationship.

Of my fellows in Livingston Hall I saw most of Elmer Beecher Russell, a University of Vermont alumnus, who roomed near me and attended many of the same courses. A taciturn Yankee with thick glasses, he was a deadly serious student whose dry sense of humor nevertheless made him agreeable company. I also came to know well Thomas Reed Powell, an older Vermont graduate, who would later be my colleague at Harvard. He was dividing his time between finishing off a doctorate in political science and teaching American constitutional law in the Law School. A very different type, Reed made up in full measure for Russ's reserve. He was a self-conscious wit, tart and irreverent in his comments, on the principle apparently that a dash of pepper always helps a stew. He loved to talk, and I had never heard anyone talk half so engagingly, though his cherished topic was himself and what he was doing and thinking. He would rap on my door about eleven at night after losing the audience which had surrounded him in the lounge; then, sprawling on my only chair, he would address me seated on the couch-bed. Sometimes my attention drifted when I thought of the unfinished work on my desk, but generally the interruption proved a welcome relief from the daily grind. Another student, Dixon Ryan Fox, who entered the Graduate School my second year, I knew only casually at the time, since Dick, a Columbia A.B., did not live in the dormitory. Neither of us dreamed that the future would see us associated in a long and exacting editorial enterprise.

Excursions into the highways and byways of the city ordinarily occurred at weekends, usually with Russ. By subway, bus, trolley, elevated, and horsecar, as well as on foot, we explored all sections of the fabulous metropolis, from Grant's Tomb on the Hudson near the head of Riverside Drive on

Morningside Heights to the Aquarium at the far harbor end of Broadway. We found there were many New Yorks: wretched Negro-jammed Harlem; the vast breathing space of Central Park with its incomparable Metropolitan Museum of Art; primly elegant Fifth Avenue; Times Square, the focus of the theatrical district; Bohemian Greenwich Village, coloring the sidewalks with paintings for sale; the polyglot East Side; enigmatic Chinatown, besides a host of others. And nearly everywhere were foreign restaurants—Oriental, German, Italian, Hungarian, and French—where we could gorge ourselves on savory food for twenty-five or thirty-five cents, the higher amount obtaining in Italian places a glass of "red ink."

The current architectural marvel in my first year was the newly opened Pennsylvania Station, "full of the noble qualities that fine and heroic imagination alone can give," as Arnold Bennett ecstatically wrote; but it was rivaled by the Grand Central Terminal of the New York Central and New Haven lines, a hardly less impressive edifice. I felt an almost proprietary interest in the Pennsylvania Station since it was my own gateway to the city. The Flatiron Building, built scarcely a decade before, was no longer a tourists' lodestone, for its twenty stories were now dwarfed by the Singer Building's forty-one and by the fifty-one of the Woolworth Building, in course of erection. In William James's phrase, "the courage, the heaven-scaling audacity of it all," made it seem hardly possible that man could ever push higher toward the stars.

During Elizabeth's first spring vacation she came on from Kalamazoo to share with me the un-Midwestern sights and experiences. She stayed with an old Columbus friend in a Barnard dormitory nearby, and as this was her introduction to New York, I acted as her guide day and night, showing her all my favorite haunts. Catching our breath between expeditions, we strolled along Riverside Drive to the soft music of the Hudson, saying the things our letters had left unsaid or only hinted, and planning with renewed confidence our future together now that I felt certain I was in the right groove.

I do not remember what shows we saw, but there must have been some. The theater held an unfailing attraction for me throughout the New York years, and I occupied a gallery seat whenever my means permitted. E. H. Sothern and Julia Marlowe in a Shakespearean cycle and Minnie Maddern Fiske and Mrs. Leslie Carter in modern plays especially stand out. I also witnessed some Gilbert and Sullivan revivals, as well as a number of contemporary musical comedies, and spent an occasional night at the newly opened Winter Garden, where Al Jolson, Frank Tinney, and other entertainers provided a mélange of skits, dancing, and songs. I even paid a single shame-faced visit to Miner's Burlesque Theater on the Bowery. It catered to all-male audiences with off-color jokes and ditties and a daring feminine seminudity which today would not raise an eyebrow of either sex. The greatest treat, and my initiation into its wonders, was grand opera. After attending the Metropolitan several times experimentally, Russ and I secured season tickets for eight Saturday evening performances and reveled in the superb voices of Caruso, Amato, Emmy Destinn, Bella Alten, and others. I formed an abiding love in particular for the works of Puccini and Wagner.

Even had I wished, it would have been hard to ignore the developments in national politics, and 1912 was a notably exciting year. My bible, the New York *Times*, despite its conservative editorial bias, provided a nonpartisan news coverage which made it possible to follow the events with ease. Teddy, having returned from a shooting trip in Africa after his presidency and taken stock of President Taft's actions, was letting fly at his erstwhile protégé for having allegedly knuckled under to the Republican reactionaries; and the Democrats were embroiled in a not unlike internal contention, with Woodrow Wilson the idol of the progressive members. Wilson, resigning as president of Princeton, had in the fall of 1910 been elected governor of New Jersey, and his policies were making a national name for him in reform circles. Moreover, standing in the wings, so to speak, were the Socialists.

Though still a minor factor, the Socialists had been rapidly gaining strength as the major parties failed to face up squarely to the issues posed by the overweening power of Big Business. One night a group of us entertained at dinner Morris Hillquit, who a few years later was to run (unsuccessfully) as Socialist candidate for mayor of New York, and I reported to Elizabeth Bancroft, "It would be difficult for any liberal to find fault with his views." Again, I joined in a long evening's discussion with Upton Sinclair, a founder of the short-lived, share-and-share-alike Helicon Hall colony at Englewood, N.J., and author of the best-selling novel *The Jungle*, which exposed the malpractices of the Chicago meat-packing industry. Ever since my youthful reading of Bellamy I had been interested in the socialist alternative to private capitalism, for it appeared a logical extension into the economic sphere of the principles of political self-government. I therefore squeezed in the course on the subject at Columbia. But neither then nor later did it seem a system that, however desirable, could be successfully accomplished overnight, for, if history teaches anything, it is that society to advance safely must make haste slowly. Nevertheless it was useful to hold up to the country a brave and clearly conceived goal, and here I believed the Socialists discharged a needed function, since the electorate unfortunately tended to shrug aside the natural-rights philosophy of its own Declaration of Independence.

Complete outsiders in the campaign, of course, were the advocates of no government at all, for the anarchists shunned political participation as an evil and their creed of direct action had long since lost them whatever wisp of a chance they had ever had to impress American opinion. Nonetheless they too conducted street meetings, and out of curiosity I attended one at which the fiery Emma Goldman spoke. "It was a strange and noisy affair," I wrote Elizabeth. "The occasion was the anniversary of the execution of Leon Czolgosz, the murderer of McKinley, whom she portrayed in heroic colors. She also defended the McNamaras in the Los Angeles dynamiting case."

Since Elizabeth was constantly prodding me about woman suffrage, I stood patiently in the hot sun one afternoon on Fifth Avenue to watch a parade which the feminists staged to influence the politicians of both old parties. "It was an impressive spectacle," I admitted to her.

It took about an hour and a half for the procession to pass, and women were walking four and sometimes eight abreast. One of the banners read: "Men bear arms, and women bear men." I couldn't help wondering how many of the marchers had actually borne men. What a shame it is to expend such immense energy on a cause that just pricks the surface of the great social questions of our time. I hope suffrage comes quickly so that people may devote attention to the real problems. I don't, however, anticipate any better political conditions from a doubling of the electorate.

As the nominating conventions drew nearer and the merits of the various aspirants became plainer, my hopes for the election—the first in which I would cast a ballot for President —centered on the triumph of the progressive elements in one or both the leading parties. When "Fighting Bob" La Follette, Wisconsin's liberal Senator, was billed to present his case to the public for the Republican candidacy in place of Taft, I waited impatiently outside Carnegie Hall for two hours, only to be finally turned away with four or five thousand others for lack of room. But I succeeded in hearing Bryan deliver a speech to Columbia students on "The Real Issue of 1912," in which the old master maintained that the times demanded someone like himself, if indeed not himself (though this he refrained from saying), to lead the Democrats to victory. A little later an undergraduate mock convention, to my delight, filled in the space which Bryan had left blank with the name of Woodrow Wilson. I greatly admired the reform measures Wilson had instituted in his state and took pride in the heartening event of a scholar in politics. Then some weeks afterward the official convention chose Wilson on the forty-sixth ballot. "I watched the *Times* bulletin board last night," I wrote Elizabeth, "and could not leave until the balloting was over. When Wilson passed the 500 mark there went up a great cheer. I have never known anything so thrilling as Bryan's part in bringing this about." The election, of course, did not occur until November, after I had left New York, when, as hardly needs saying, the Democrats overwhelmed Taft, his strength having been undermined by Roosevelt, the standard-bearer of the newly formed Progressive party.

My unexpected second year in the Graduate School had resulted from a fellowship which paid a few hundred dollars above tuition. This carried the obligation of writing my doctoral thesis with Osgood. The only fellowship in American history at the time lay alternately within his gift and that of Dunning, and Osgood's turn had now come. Despite my admiration for his conscientious scholarship I had hoped to work with Beard on some aspect of the national period, but my financial situation permitted no choice and, when Osgood suggested the appointment, I accepted, though with one reservation: that he not put me on an institutional study of a single colony, which had been his way of having students supplement his own researches. Quietly consenting after a moment, he proposed instead an investigation of the so-called Continental Association, the comprehensive boycott of imports and exports which the patriots instituted in 1774 to force concessions from Britain. This banished any further hesitation, since the topic offered an opportunity to examine the interrelation of economics and politics, something which Beard had so deeply interested me in.

That summer upon going back to Xenia I made a head start

on the project. Miss McElwain, now in a library building of her own erected with Carnegie money, borrowed from the State University the six bulky volumes of Peter Force's *American Archives* for the years 1774-76 and set aside a room in the basement for my use. This remarkable compilation of newspaper excerpts and other contemporary records yielded a treasure-trove of notes, but also convinced me that the theme as Professor Osgood had envisaged it was too narrow. The Continental Association, far from standing alone, was in fact the culmination of a series of nonintercourse pacts which had begun a decade before. Henceforth this larger movement became my subject. In the study as eventually completed, the original topic occupied only six of the fifteen chapters.

Returning to Columbia in the autumn for my final year, I shelved my researches for the time in order to meet the residence requirements for the doctorate. In mid-October I disposed of the language tests—sight translations of Latin, French, and German—and from then on, except for attending classes, I prepared for the further ordeal, the general examination in subject matter. Glimpses of my tribulations—commonplace to any doctoral candidate at this stage—appear in letters to Elizabeth: "I hardly know how to tackle the great mass of knowledge that still stands between me and a successful outcome" (March 21, 1912); "I'm so sick of cramming my head with facts and theories and views. I get enthusiastic over my work when I have reports to write, but the kind of mental training I am now going through is deadening" (April 16); "I have been spending my time today with Aristotle, Cleanthes, Epictetus, Plutarch and a few others of that sort" (April 20); "I have just returned from a quiz that three of us who are to be examined hold each week" (April 25).

At last, on May 9, I faced my inquisitors, a dozen or so members of the faculty. Professor Osgood, who presided, considerately put me at ease with an initial question which even a high-school pupil—in those days—could have answered

("What was the date of the Quebec Act?"). Though his later questions and those of his colleagues proved genuinely searching, none seemed unreasonable, and the two hours passed almost before I knew it. "I am just out of the examination," I wrote to Elizabeth, "and I enjoyed the experience as much or more than the examiners did. Really the suspense and the long grind of the preparation were the worst features." A few days later I added: "So far as I have been able to learn, I am the only candidate for the Ph.D. who is only two years out of college. I feel very fortunate in getting started so young."

A further boost to my spirits arose from the assurance of a teaching position, for Professor Knight some months before had offered me an instructorship at Ohio State, to begin in the fall. The salary, $900, was low even for that time, but in terms of purchasing power today it was probably equivalent to $2,000 or $2,500. With this worry removed, I stayed on in the East during the summer to gather more data for my thesis, spending some weeks at the New York Public Library and the New-York Historical Society, then moving on to the rich collections in and about Boston. Much more remained to be done in Boston, however, and I needed further to explore the holdings in the South Atlantic states. The road to the Ph.D. was still to be a long one.

IV

Entering the Academic Profession

The return to Ohio State in a new capacity involved a variety of adjustments, making me in some sense feel a stranger in the familiar surroundings. Above everything else, of course, it meant a practical testing of my choice of a career. I was now to sit at the opposite side of the desk and could not help wondering whether I would make good. Though knowing how to assemble the raw material for the classroom, would I be able to pass the knowledge on intelligibly and interestingly to others? The answer to this was vital. A quite different adaptation entailed a change in the pleasant living arrangements of my undergraduate years. Hugo and Mary had now moved to the east end of Columbus, several miles from the campus, so to be near my duties I found quarters in a lodging house where other bachelor instructors roomed, and ate as a rule at the Ohio Union, the recently opened student social center. Besides, I faced an altered relationship with former teachers, now my colleagues, as well as with other members of the faculty; but this fortunately proved no problem. They could hardly have greeted me more cordially or taken greater pains to put me at my ease. As a matter of course, however, most of my time was spent with the unmarried ones; and three of them, though ten years or more older than I and of professorial rank, became valued friends.

Francis W. Coker in political science had a quiet, remorseless way of challenging loose statements that taught me to be more sure of my own ground before speaking. He was a recent addition from the Princeton staff, with his major interest in political theory, and his deliberate enunciation betrayed his South Carolina birth. Frank outstayed me at Ohio State by a decade, then moved on to a chair at Yale. In contrast Alonzo H. Tuttle, who taught constitutional law in the Law College, dearly loved talk for its own sake, playing with ideas just for the fun of it, and there were few matters in which he was not interested. Although essentially an onlooker of life, he surprisingly forsook the role for two years by serving in the State Senate, with decided benefit to the University in the form of appropriations for a badly needed new library. Henry Spencer, who had kept a fatherly eye on me as an undergraduate, was on leave the first year, after which he also was one of the group. In looking back I wonder why they admitted me to the circle. Perhaps it was because, while sharing their generally liberal social outlook, I sometimes enlivened the exchanges with somewhat more advanced views.

My most colorful colleague, though one I saw less of, was Ludwig Lewisohn, a professor of German, whose rich cultivation and literary gifts far transcended the field of his instruction. His wife, moreover—destined to be the first of several—wrote plays under the name of "Bosworth Crocker." They lived near me, and to enter their home was somewhat like going from Morningside Heights to Greenwich Village. They observed no regular eating or sleeping hours, shunned academic parties because, in Lewisohn's words, "people only sent their clothes and left their real selves at home," and scandalized the neighborhood by noisily entertaining callers late into the night. As a further sign of individuality they sometimes neglected their grocery bills, and on at least one occasion President Thompson advanced the money to stave off court proceedings. Lewisohn left the University, at the same time I did, for a position on the *Nation*; and a few years later, from the vantage ground of New York, he published his autobiographical book *Up Stream*, which pronounced vitriolic judgment on the bourgeois Ohio State community and all its works. He wrote off both faculty and students as, by and large, spineless conformists and portrayed his benefactor Thompson as possessing "the intellectual equipment of a Presbyterian elder" with "the aesthetic and philosophic vision of the Saturday Evening Post." Undoubtedly Lewisohn and the University shared the blame for his unhappy experience.

Another unconventional character, though I did not realize it then, was John H. Snook, a burly, florid-faced assistant professor of veterinary medicine with whom Frank Coker and I sometimes happened to eat at the Ohio Union. His academic field hardly suggests romance, and whether he had already ventured on a secret love life I do not know; but several years after I went away from Columbus he murdered his pregnant secretary in order to prevent her from exposing him to his wife. The bungling Don Juan thereupon exchanged his University seat for the electric chair; and the administration, as though fearing his fate did not provide sufficient warning, decreed that thenceforward the upper half of office doors in campus buildings should be of transparent glass.

My teaching load consisted of the usual thirteen hours a week, with the first class at eight in the morning. I gave two sections of introductory American history and another for beginners in political science plus two subjects of an advanced character. One, The American Revolution and the Confederation Period, I felt adequately equipped to offer on the basis of my Columbia training, but for the other, Jurisprudence, I had absolutely no preparation. Regularly taught by Spencer, it fell temporarily to me because of his absence that year and everyone else's unwillingness to take it on. I, of course, had no choice. Not infrequently I skated on very thin ice, and the students had good reason to think they were getting less out of it than they should. The elementary course on the United States, my major assignment, still used the *Epochs of American History* as the textbook just as when I was an undergraduate, and by an interesting coincidence we reached Woodrow Wilson's volume on March 4, 1913, the very day he entered the White House to make history on his own. In subsequent years the text was John Spencer Bassett's newly published *Short History of the United States* which, though belying the adjective, possessed the merit of incorporating the latest scholarly knowledge as well as of bringing the story down to date. It was an encyclopedestrian account, however; and because it was also confusingly organized in places, my senior colleague Homer Hockett and I got out a printed syllabus to put the treatment in better order and introduce references to helpful collateral reading. Soon students began asking why we did not write our own book, and in the end that is what we did, though various interruptions delayed its completion until after I had quit the scene.

After the first few years I dropped the teaching of political science to devote all my time to United States history, gradually taking on at the Department's suggestion additional advanced courses on The Civil War and Reconstruction, on Diplomatic History, and on The History of Political Parties. Knight and Hockett continued to give the only seminars. In an effort to break away from orthodox subject matter I secured permission, however, in my seventh and last year to offer in the summer school a course for teachers on Some Revisions of American History. This, having no stated boundaries, made it possible to deal with aspects of the nation's past which the standard accounts ignored or slighted. It went so well I was encouraged to think that here lay the possibility of another book.

Although I was not much older than most of my students, they did not seem to notice it, and soon I did not either. At the beginning I endeavored to model myself on some of my own greatly admired professors but quickly learned it was better to be myself. It is always difficult to see ourselves as others see us, but nearly half a century later James Thurber cast some light on the matter. "I remember," he said in a syndicated interview in the New York *Post*, June 8, 1959, "on the last day of a history class at Ohio State in 1914, after the bell had rung, Professor Arthur Schlesinger, Sr.—the old man —saying, 'Mr. Spencer, who is President of the United States?' Mr. Spencer said, 'Woodrow Wilson.' Professor Schlesinger said, 'Thank you! I was determined that you get one question right this year.'" This is a reminder that, as is so common with young instructors, I, too, readily indulged in sarcasm, a fault which, however, in due time I outgrew. A reminiscence of a different kind came in a letter from a former Ohio State student in New York City upon hearing of my retirement from the Harvard faculty. He recalled seeing me run to class "with full, even strides," getting there "just an eyelash past eight o'clock." This struck him as such an amazing feat by a presumably sedate member of the faculty that he wrote it up for the *Lantern*, from which, he said, one of the press associations spread it through the country.

Whenever possible I stole time for further work on my doctoral thesis, using materials at hand in the University Library. But the major unfinished business necessitated return trips to the East—to Boston, Philadelphia, Baltimore, Charleston, S.C., and Washington—and to that I devoted the summers of 1913 and 1914. Two memories apart from the grubbing for data linger from my Boston stay. One is of rooming in a loosely screened house in Cambridge where I waged nightly battle with swarms of mosquitoes until I at last fended them off by arching over my pillow half of a barrel hoop covered with netting. The other is of meeting Harvard's Professor Edward

Channing, who was consulting manuscripts at the Massachusetts Historical Society for the fourth volume of his *History of the United States*. Short and rotund with protuberant blue eyes and ruddy cheeks, he was not at all the imposing figure I had imagined. When he learned I was an Osgood disciple, he drew himself up and snorted, "Osgood does not approve of me. He thinks me too flippant, too much of a Bernard Shaw." Later, as Channing's colleague, I discovered that his bark was always worse than his bite. Indeed, I sensed this earlier, for one of the first letters of congratulation upon my thesis came from him.

Everywhere but Charleston the custodians of source materials proved helpful beyond the call of duty. There the Library Society, possessing an important collection of Southern colonial newspapers and pamphlets, kept open only short hours, and the prim old gentlewomen in charge forbade visitors in spite of the sweltering heat to doff their coats. Besides, the boardinghouse nearby where I ate served its main meal, a heavy and soporific one, at three in the afternoon. These circumstances did nothing to expedite my labors beyond determining me to push on as quickly as possible.

In Washington, happily, I was able to combine business with pleasure, since Elizabeth Bancroft was at hand. Her mother some months before had transferred from the Columbus branch of the Pension Bureau to the main office in the capital; and when I finished my daily stint at the Library of Congress, with Elizabeth sometimes assisting me, we would explore the city and—much more to the point—we at last fixed the date for our marriage. As my salary had risen from $1,000 in the past year to a budgeted $1,200 for the coming one, there seemed no occasion for further delay. Then, just a few weeks before the time set, Professor Knight in the role of a good fairy wrote that the figure had been increased to $1,500, with promotion to an assistant professorship. Now indeed we felt we were in clover. The wedding took place on September 5,

1914, at a Congregational minister's study in the presence of Mrs. Bancroft and a few friends, after which we went off to Atlantic City for several days to bask in the sun and get acquainted on a new basis. On arriving in Columbus for the opening of the academic year I had less than a dollar in my pocketbook.

In the first four years together we lived in as many different places. Starting in a small furnished apartment rented at nominal cost from a woman professor on leave, we next found ampler quarters in half of a double house, then moved into a whole one, and, finally, with the help of a large mortgage, acquired an attractive stucco-and-timber residence of our own. As we had hoped, our home proved a magnet for our friends, both those on the faculty and Elizabeth's from Columbus days. Perhaps our demonstration of happiness encouraged Frank Coker to take the plunge, which he did in July, 1916. By that time we had a coed living with us to assist with the housework; and as I received successive pay raises and was promoted in 1917 to full professor at a salary of $2,250 with an additional $250 the next year, all our circumstances became easier. Our one sadness was the loss of our first child, Katharine, born on September 27, 1915, who died of an intestinal ailment ten months later. This made all the more welcome the arrival of Arthur Bancroft Schlesinger on October 15, 1917.

Though I had finished the research on my thesis the summer of our marriage, the writing required nearly three years more. It proceeded fastest during the summers, since I could work on it only at odd hours while teaching. I had never before tackled so large and complex a subject, but as I studied and restudied the data, the material gradually fell into order. After composing and revising each chapter in longhand, I would perhaps rephrase it again while copying it off on my secondhand typewriter. Elizabeth recalls that when she had to be out I would sometimes type with Katharine in my lap. By June, 1915, the first draft was in shape, but it took until March,

1917, to prepare the final version. I named it *The Colonial Merchants and the American Revolution, 1763-1776* for want of a better title, and with some trepidation dispatched it to Professor Osgood. He considered it, he wrote, "a very fine piece of work," but had reservations about the punctuation and thought the first two chapters needed retouching to present a less favorable view of the British commercial system. Beard, the second reader, approved it without change.

I met Osgood's criticisms, and on his initiative the Columbia University Press brought out the study, with a subsidy of $250 from me, in an edition of 1,000 copies. Osgood further made it possible for me to take the final examination for the doctorate, an oral defense of the thesis, on the way to a meeting of the American Historical Association at Philadelphia late in December. By then—a matter I shall return to—the United States had been in World War I for eight months; zero weather gripped Columbus; coal stood in short supply for civilians; and our own bin was down to a mere half a ton, with no definite assurance from our dealer of more. So it was with deep anxiety for the well-being of Elizabeth and our infant son that I headed east, though, as it fortunately turned out, the supply came a few days later. The examination itself presented no difficulty because in the nature of things I knew more about the subject than my questioners. The following June the degree was formally awarded.

The *Colonial Merchants*, dedicated to my parents, combined, I liked to think, the research methods of Osgood with the insights of Beard; but Beard had warned me against mentioning him in the preface because, having by that time published his controversial *Economic Interpretation of the Constitution*, he wrote that his name was "a red flag to the historical bull." Though having no choice but to obey his wishes, I doubt that any harm could have resulted. In concentrating on the economic causes I carefully noted in the foreword that "the revolutionary movement was the product of a complexity of

forces, governmental and personal, British and colonial, social, economic, geographical and religious," each of which
must be properly assessed to arrive at a definitive account.
Beard with fantastic overstatement hailed the book in the
New Republic as "the most significant contribution that has
ever been made to the history of the American Revolution,"
and from the standpoint of methodology I was equally
elated to have Charles M. Andrews, Yale's colonial authority,
cite it in the *American Historical Review* as "a model of creative research." The American Historical Association awarded
it the Justin Winsor Prize. Despite the fact that the acceptance of its findings by subsequent students of the Revolution
seemingly destroyed its further usefulness, it continued to be
in sufficient demand to be twice reprinted independently of
the Columbia University Press, in 1939 and in 1957.

I did not ask myself at the time, but I have often done so
since, whether the six years spent in securing the doctorate
after meeting the residence requirements did not unduly pro-
long my novitiate. Certainly a representative segment of the
study—say, the first five of the fifteen chapters—would have
adequately demonstrated the capacity to search out evidence
and reach valid conclusions, and this would have greatly
shortened the period. But under the regulations then in force
even such a portion would have had to be submitted in print,
and that I was unwilling to do inasmuch as the whole comprised a seamless story. On the other hand, the thesis as finally
presented was undoubtedly a more mature product than it
would otherwise have been. Under the later and sounder
Columbia system one would not have had to face these alternatives. In my case, though, whatever it may have been in that
of others, the delay did not, I think, actually hold back my
academic career.

Notwithstanding the preoccupation with my thesis I managed some writing on the side. In 1916, to help out a civil-en-
gineering professor who with a Michigan representative had

just resurveyed the once violently disputed Ohio-Michigan boundary, I unraveled the origins of the controversy as part of the published report of their findings. I also joined several colleagues in issuing and providing material for the *Ohio History Teachers' Journal*, which we conducted for a few years. Then, when a batch of youthful letters of Salmon P. Chase came to the Ohio State Archaeological and Historical Society, I edited the correspondence for its *Quarterly*. This, however, was in 1919, after the *Colonial Merchants* was behind me. Two further articles stemmed from papers prepared for the American Historical Association. The first, "The Uprising against the East India Company," at the Cincinnati gathering in 1916, maintained, contrary to the then orthodox belief, that "the fear of monopoly," not the principle of no taxation without representation, lay behind the Boston Tea Party and related colonial acts of opposition. The second, "The American Revolution Reconsidered," intended for the Cleveland meeting in 1918, presented the newer viewpoints on the period as a whole; but that assemblage, along with those of other scholarly organizations, was called off because of the government's wartime transportation requirements. Both essays subsequently appeared in the *Political Science Quarterly*, and both, needless to say, grew out of the work on my thesis.

Aside from offering a forum for budding scholars, the Historical Association's annual conventions afforded an opportunity to listen to the papers of eminent members and to become personally acquainted with them. In that way I early met Frederick Jackson Turner, who by now had transferred from Wisconsin to Harvard; and this resulted in an occasion, thrilling to a novice in the profession, when it fell to me to introduce Turner and Beard to each other. Oddly, these two men, advocating as they did rival interpretations of American history, had never before come face to face. And, when I myself advanced in the profession and was in turn sought out, I discovered that the benefit did not lie only in the one direction, for acquaintance with younger men kept me informed of the interests of the oncoming generation.

In national affairs, as has been noted in passing, these years at Ohio State coincided with the eventful era of Woodrow Wilson and our participation in World War I. In Coker I found a fellow Wilson enthusiast, for Frank had served under him at Princeton and had warmed to Wilson's program of keeping the social and athletic "sideshows" from "swallowing up the circus." On the night of the 1912 election we breathlessly followed the telegraphic reports with Tuttle at a club downtown. "It is only nine o'clock," I took time off to scribble to Elizabeth, then, of course, still in Kalamazoo,

but the returns already indicate a tremendous victory for Wilson. . . . I voted early this morning and cast votes for Democratic, Republican, Progressive and Socialist nominees. I am inclined to think that this may be my last national Democratic vote and that next time I shall either be voting Progressive (if anyone but Roosevelt is nominated) or Socialist. But many things may happen in four years.

And many things did. Despite my initial doubts of Wilson's capacity to weld his amorphous following into an effective instrument for reform, he pushed through Congress an impressive sheaf of domestic measures which robbed both the Progressives and the Socialists of their liberal appeal. Moreover, by wielding what he called "the sword of penetrating speech," Wilson, though lacking the later advantage of radio and television, lifted the crucial issues above mere partisan considerations for the rank and file. Time and again men whom I came to know in later years said that they had switched permanently to the Democratic party at this period. I did not, however, lose interest in socialism as a theory and yeast for thought; and when John Spargo and Rose Pastor Stokes spoke to the undergraduate Intercollegiate Socialist Society, each spent the night with us. Spargo, a former Welsh miner, was a polished expositor of Marxism; no one could then have guessed that in the 1920's he would turn into a Republican of the Coolidge-Hoover brand. By contrast, Mrs. Stokes, a Russian Jewish immigrant girl who had married a wealthy New York Socialist, relied on her striking looks and emotional fervor; she ended up in after years a Communist. What strange fruit the identical tree bore!

From July, 1914, when the European war erupted, it dwelt more or less constantly in all our minds. In the early stages, though, it seemed of no direct concern to America, just the same old power struggle across the seas. Accordingly I welcomed Wilson's plea to be "impartial in thought as well as in action." Even more, I responded enthusiastically to his vision of a league of nations to prevent like catastrophes in the future. But, as the conflict went on, I grew increasingly impatient with Wilson's extraordinary forbearance in dealing with infringements of neutrality, especially those by Germany, the grosser offender; and these actions, together with Germany's ruthless methods of land warfare, convinced me that her triumph would imperil America's own security and way of life. Nevertheless I voted for Wilson again in 1916, for, though his supporters dinned the slogan "He kept us out of war," he himself made clear in speeches at Cincinnati and elsewhere that he would not continue the policy of peace at any price, whereas Hughes, the Republican standard-bearer, commanded ardent pro-German backing and said nothing that might alienate it until almost the end of the campaign.

The majority of the faculty, I think, took satisfaction in Wilson's re-election, the most notable exception being Ludwig Lewisohn, whose attachment to Germany reflected, not approval of her militarism, but love of her literature and music. On visits to Xenia I found, too, that my father, now nearing seventy, was strongly pro-German. Like so many other citizens of Teutonic birth he harbored a romantic notion of a *Vaterland* he had known only as a child. Father argued that America by taking up arms would merely be a dupe of England. But when the unrestricted German submarine campaign plunged the United States into the struggle in April, 1917, he unhesitatingly took his stand with the country of his children against the land of his forefathers. As he said with an economy of words, "It is now our fight." Lewisohn, however, proved irreconcilable to the end. So came about America's renewed involvement in war, something which I and my fellow cadets not so many years before had confidently believed could never, never, happen again.

As an ill-prepared nation girded for the fray the University sought by every means possible to contribute to the effort. Many undergraduates left at once to enlist; and with others enrolling in the Students' Army Training Corps to fit themselves for officer positions while still in college, the scene took on a grim martial look. Youngsters in khaki now purposefully strode the campus where boys in blue had before played at being soldiers. Faculty departures involved mostly men in engineering and medicine, but Tuttle acted during the summer of 1918 as a legal consultant in Washington on war matters, and Spencer served for the duration with the Army Y.M.C.A. in Italy. We stay-at-homes fretted and stewed and tried in our own small way to further the cause. I registered for the draft, as required by law, but the contest did not last long enough to call up fathers. To save food for the armed forces, Elizabeth saw that we faithfully heeded the nationwide appeal for "meatless meals" and "wheatless days," and I spaded up the back yard to grow our own beans, corn, peas, tomatoes, and other edibles. This venture in civilian trench warfare, as Tuttle dubbed it, proved so enjoyable in itself that I have never since been without a vegetable patch, though it has usually been on a less ambitious scale. We also bought Liberty Bonds up to and beyond our ability.

Desiring to do something suited to my professional training, I proposed to Governor James M. Cox the establishment of an official body to gather data on Ohio's participation in the conflict. The resulting Ohio Historical Commission, under

my chairmanship, consisted largely of history professors scattered through the state. Operating from headquarters at the
Ohio State Archaeological and Historical Society on the campus, we set up county branches to co-operate in obtaining
records of local military and civilian activities and secured
free subscriptions from newspapers to supplement the information. In the end we assembled a mass of printed and manuscript materials which might otherwise have been lost. Our
collection of soldier newspapers from the several Ohio camps
prompted me after the war to write a more general article
on the subject of "The Khaki Journalists" for the *Mississippi
Valley Historical Review.*

As the hostilities were drawing toward a close, a letter from
John Spargo invited me to attend on October 3 a conference
in Chicago of liberals who, having lost faith in the existing
parties, were seeking a new political alignment. Spargo himself had quit the Socialist party when it denounced America's
resort to arms. My own unhappiness derived from the feeling
that the crusade for democracy abroad was being marred by
its growing eclipse at home. An irrational hatred of everything
German had swept the country, reducing the enrollment in
the University's German courses, for example, from around
1,000 to 149 after we entered the fight, and the Wilson government itself under Attorney General Palmer had engaged fran-
tically in the suppression of freedom of speech. Besides pro-
war Socialists, the two-day meeting brought together former
Progressives left stranded by Roosevelt's return to the Republican fold in 1916, disaffected Democrats, and independents
of various kinds, even some single-taxers and Prohibitionists
dissatisfied with the adequacy of their traditional panaceas.
The outcome was a statement of principles declaring for political, economic, and international democracy and the forma-
tion of the Committee of Forty-Eight (meaning hopefully by
that all the then states) to promote a new national party.
There was even talk about a name for it, with a preference for

"Commonweal" until someone pointed out that the members would be called Common Squealers. No major political figure was present, and as a student of American history I should have known that the movement, handicapped by the electorate's attachment to accustomed loyalties, could not possibly succeed without experienced direction. In fact even Teddy's ably led Progressive party had proved but a flash in the pan. Upon cooler thought, indeed, I came to this conclusion and took no part in any subsequent conferences. In the meantime, however, under the spell of the gathering I delivered speeches on behalf of the cause to labor groups and church brotherhoods in Columbus. The resulting publicity led both Professor Knight and President Thompson to seek me out and shake their heads dubiously over this activity.

Another incident some months afterward did nothing to enhance my reputation for discreet behavior with the University powers. Inside the academic community the cessation of fighting in November, 1918, brought to a head the problem of the high cost of living. Soaring wartime prices had overtaken faculty salaries, especially in the case of the junior ranks. After waiting until late in the winter for the administration to evince concern, a few of us called a meeting of several hundred of our colleagues, and they with bitter comments adopted resolutions demanding that the president immediately obtain the necessary legislative appropriations. This display of insurgency was an untoward event which in the minds of the authorities cast discredit upon the ringleaders. As a matter of fact, however, the episode produced no results. Ohio State was to trail a year or so behind other Midwestern state universities in upgrading its pay.

Meanwhile I had left the institution. In the spring of 1919 a dean from the University of Iowa appeared in Columbus in search of a head for his History Department, and Knight gave me such a glowing recommendation that President Walter A. Jessup invited me to Iowa City for an interview. The upshot was an offer of $3,500—an increase of $1,000 over my Ohio State salary—with the freedom to teach any courses I chose, including the direction of graduate students, an opportunity hitherto denied me. It did not mar my pleasure in accepting to suspect I was being kicked upstairs. On the personal side, of course, Elizabeth and I grieved at parting with good friends. We recognized, however, as did they, that this was the cost inherent in so nomadic a profession.

V

The Iowa Interlude

Iowa City, my academic home from 1919 to 1924, was a place of some 11,000 souls situated in gently rolling prairie country in the heart of a rich agricultural community. Once the town had been the territorial seat of government. Now it existed largely by grace of the University. The teaching staff and maintenance force plus the annual influx of six or seven thousand students provided the chief means of its livelihood. The discarded gray stone capitol, its classical symmetry overtopped by barrack-like but dignified classroom buildings, stood at the center of the campus, housing the administrative officials. An array of small stores and two hotels adjoined the grounds, and there were also two struggling dailies in addition to the college newspaper. To be adequately informed the citizens had to take Des Moines or Chicago papers. Automobiles for pleasure driving were few, for one could easily go about on foot in town, while the dirt country roads almost prohibited motoring in wet weather and reeked with dust in dry. No theaters were to be found, and the three movie houses offered only silent films in this era before photography acquired a voice. As for the newfangled radio, it was admittedly an interesting toy, but the programs were too poor and the reception too uncertain to give it wide favor.

The residential streets, arched with elms and oaks and lined by modest dwellings with deep back yards, vividly recalled the Xenia of my boyhood. We lived the first year in the Unitarian parsonage during the absence of the minister, then purchased our own place, an old-fashioned frame house which sufficiently met our needs but, as we presently found, was jerry-built. On one occasion, when the English historian J. Holland Rose stayed overnight, we discovered to our chagrin that he had had to stuff the rattling window frames with newspapers in order to sleep. It was here that our second son, Thomas Bancroft, was born on June 9, 1922, Arthur being then nearly five. In the meantime the Schlesinger family back in Ohio had begun to fall away. Olga died in 1915 of Addison's disease while I was still in Columbus; Father, long in declining health, and Hugo, prematurely, followed in 1920. Hugo, but forty-two and serving as county prosecuting attorney, was running for election as probate judge when a blood clot induced by an appendicitis operation carried him off. With his grasp of governmental affairs and his personal gifts he had appeared destined to go far in the public life of the state and even of the nation.

Though Elizabeth and I went to Iowa City as total strangers, my new colleagues at once made us feel thoroughly at home. In a short while it seemed as though we had known them for years. In so small a world we met them daily in the streets. Moreover, the faculty community, driven in on itself by the dearth of other outlets, compensated by entertaining lavishly and often. Accustomed as we were to relative privacy, we sometimes had the sensation of living in a fishbowl. Dinner parties were both large and elaborate, the guests frequently distributed through several rooms and always in formal dress. This was not at all what we from the older Middle West, vaguely thinking of Iowa as still in the frontier stage, had expected. The same two middle-aged sisters catered at all the functions, making us at first wonder why every accommodator in Iowa City looked alike. The Eighteenth Amendment, going into effect our first year, cast no pall on these affairs, since the Hawkeye state had long had prohibition, and none of our acquaintances showed the slightest desire to infringe the national ban.

Academically the University displayed a pleasing contrast to Ohio State. There, I had felt the lack of a considered overall aim, a tendency to drift with the tide; but Iowa, under President Jessup's vigorous leadership, had a well-defined purpose as well as a clear-cut program. The purpose was to place the University through its Extension Service and other means immediately at the disposal of all the people. The program was to offer on the campus a wide range of instruction in the liberal arts and the professions, both to broaden the students' intellectual horizons and to equip them for satisfying and useful careers. Unlike Ohio State, agriculture and the related subjects were taught elsewhere, at the land-grant college in Ames.

Jessup, a stocky, square-jawed man who looked and acted more like a business executive or banker than a university president, had held office since a year before the war; now, thanks to the retirement or death of a number of department heads and his success in obtaining increased postwar appropriations ahead of other state universities, he had lured scholars away from rival institutions, I being but the youngest of the lot. In this fashion he reorganized five other departments in addition to History, and the injection of fresh blood had a tonic effect throughout the faculty. From as far away as Yale, Professor Max Farrand wrote me, "Almost everyone is being attracted and being impressed by the various groups of workers that are gathered at the University of Iowa, and everything that has been done is watched with favorable eyes."

Jessup, however, wielded the reins with an ever vigilant eye on the legislature. This was first borne in on me shortly after arriving, when Jessup at the prompting of a lawmaker quizzed me about the Committee of Forty-Eight and was visibly relieved to learn I had ceased connection with it. And some months later, after the History Department included the Covenant of the League of Nations in *Great Charters of Americanism,* a booklet of documents published under my editorship, protests poured in on him from all over this bitterly isolationist state. In retrospect, I am bound to admit, the outcry had merit, for the Covenant was still being debated in the Senate, which was presently to reject it. The University to its credit, though suspending further distribution, did not withdraw the objectionable insertion until the Senate had taken final action. I summed up Jessup's philosophy of the relation of faculty members to public issues in response to a letter from Upton Sinclair, who was then gathering material on the invisible influences controlling American education for his book *The Goose-Step.* "His position," I said,

is a purely pragmatic one. Since his main job is to get funds from the state legislature, he does not propose to allow the indiscretions of a professor to damage the cause of the University there. . . . He would even protect a professor from outside criticism, up to a certain point. But if appropriations are involved, then his allegiance is to the appropriation. But in justice to the president I must add that no alleged radical has been dismissed from the faculty.

One of the academic newcomers, Hardin Craig from the University of Minnesota, became a warm friend. The head of the English Department, he was an authority on Shakespeare, particularly concerned with the ideas about man and nature in the Elizabethan age which had influenced the great playwright's conception of his characters. But, this apart, he had wide-ranging intellectual interests and was a gifted raconteur with a special knack for telling Negro folk stories remembered from his Kentucky childhood. On Sunday mornings we would tramp the country roads, bowing low from time to time before the tall corn or the fat porkers in recognition of the twin foundations of Iowa's wealth and the University's income. Frequently we were joined by Herbert F. Goodrich, a law professor who, like Craig, was well informed outside his own field and provided a further dimension to the exchanges. Both outstayed me on the faculty, Craig eventually going to Stanford, while Goodrich moved on first to the University of Michigan, then to the deanship of law at Pennsylvania, and, finally, to a judgeship of a United States Circuit Court in that state.

Perhaps the most challenging intellect I encountered was Frank H. Knight, later of the University of Chicago, who specialized in economic theory. In the spirit of John Stuart Mill he accepted no doctrine "without a rigid scrutiny by negative criticism" and insisted "upon having the meaning of a word clearly understood before using it." The impression he gave of thinking out loud reminded me of my old professor James Harvey Robinson. Among other things Knight helped clarify my conception of the economic interpretation of history by stressing that economic motives were not, and could not be, a mere mechanical factor, since people were just as apt to follow their supposed interests as their real ones and thus, in fact, go against their material advantage. I had not hitherto been blind to this, but Knight's cogent way of putting it lodged it in the foreground of my mind.

The faculty, of course, contained its share of unusual characters, who perhaps stood out more prominently than elsewhere because the academic community lived so much to itself. There was the gentle little professor of chemistry dominated by a large masculine wife, who recovered his manliness after her death by marrying a deaf-and-dumb woman. There was the economics professor whose voice, the dean had said in advance of his coming, would "be heard all over the United States" and certainly could be heard all over the building where he lectured. There was the absent-minded professor of psychology who on taking off his clothes to dress for a party went to bed instead. There was, besides, the professor of literature who was cured of the habit of saying to his class, "To put it all in a nutshell . . . ," by overhearing a student say, "Oh, what a nut!" There was the wife who, according to a faculty wit, "glamored for attention" and possessed "lots of wile power." There was the professor—indeed, more than one— who, playing golf every afternoon, complained of lack of time to write that never-finished book. And in my own Department one of the older members had a way of threatening to kill himself when his wishes were denied, until at last I suggested he do as he thought best. Meanwhile I had read it was not in the nature of suicides to proclaim their intentions.

Outside the University I was likely to seek the company of Frank Doan, the Unitarian clergyman whose house we had occupied the first year. Ethical in his outlook rather than religious in the conventional sense, he displayed not the least concern at my unwillingness to accept teachings which defied intellectual proof. In a quiet, self-effacing manner he always sought to fortify the finer instincts of people regardless of their formal professions. Oddly enough, I do not think I ever heard him preach, but I seldom left him without feeling spiritually refreshed.

In my own Department I had anticipated difficulty because two of the senior professors, both much older than I, had desired the headship. In fact, however, each was so gratified by the discomfiture of the other that they gave me loyal support. They and their fellow members were good teachers but had little heart for investigation on their own. To repair this weakness it was necessary to bring in promising younger men in the junior ranks. The University, lacking positions to which to promote them, could not keep them long, but meanwhile they evidenced their zest for research and writing. In this manner we acquired the services of such youthful scholars of later distinction as Raymond J. Sontag, subsequently at Princeton and the University of California at Berkeley; Ralph E. Turner, ultimately on the Yale faculty; and John H. Wuorinen, now at

Columbia. Walther I. Brandt, a Wisconsin Ph.D. in United States history, affords an especially interesting case. The Library had recently obtained a set of the *Monumenta Germaniae Historica,* and since we had no Medieval specialist and Brandt was the only one on our staff with an easy reading knowledge of German, I offered to reduce his teaching schedule for a year if he would prepare himself to transfer to that period. Henceforth, both at Iowa and afterward at New York University, he made the Middle Ages his field.

For my part, I at first repeated the courses on American Diplomatic History and The History of Political Parties, given at Ohio State, adding one on Recent American History (since 1870) and a graduate seminar in that period. In the summer of 1920 I also taught the course on Some Revisions of American History—now retitled New Viewpoints in American History—for the second and last time. Then in the third year, 1922-23, I realized a long-cherished ambition by introducing a course on The Social and Cultural History of the United States (in lieu of the one on Political Parties) and began devoting my seminars to that field. This, so far as I know, was the first instruction ever offered in any college or university on that phase of our past. The Iowa undergraduates did not differ noticeably from those at Ohio State except that, being more inclined to regard higher education as a privilege and opportunity instead of a right, they generally worked harder. For most of them Iowa City itself, small though it was, proved an enlightening experience, since they typically came from farms or crossroads villages. The University Librarian complained of the mutilating of books and attributed it to the fact that the offenders had never before used a lending library.

Not having earlier offered graduate work, I could not compare the two institutions in this respect, but in ability and seriousness of purpose the students measured up well to those I was later to have at Harvard. Five doctoral theses fell to me in the five years. One, by Bessie L. Pierce, who helped give the elementary American history while instructing in the College of Education, was published by Knopf under the title *Public Opinion and the Teaching of History*. It surveyed the hitherto uninvestigated subject from colonial times onward. Another by Fred A. Shannon, *The Organization and Administration of the Union Army*, brought out by the Arthur H. Clark Company, won both the American Historical Association's Justin Winsor Prize and the Pulitzer Prize. Miss Pierce and Shannon in due course became professors respectively at the University of Chicago and the University of Illinois.

As a representative of the Graduate School one year I visited various colleges of the state to lecture on a subject designed to interest students in continuing their education beyond the baccalaureate degree. My theme was "The Role of the Newspapers in the American Revolution," a matter which had aroused my interest when working on the *Colonial Merchants* and on which, though I as yet had no thought of it, I would eventually write a book. Of the thirty institutions, I spoke at fifteen. To reach some of them posed a real problem because the railroads running north and south were few and primitive. In going to Luther College at Decorah in northeastern Iowa, for instance, I had to take a bumpy, single-track, narrow-gauge line. The temperature was below zero; the handful of passengers, swathed in fur caps, overcoats, wool mufflers, and mittens, derived little comfort from the coal stove at the end of the car; and at every stopping place we all rushed out to huddle for the time around the blazing station stove. But my welcome on arriving more than made up for the discomfort.

These colleges had as a rule been founded by religious denominations and once been thriving institutions, but with the changing times and the growth of the state university a number had fallen upon evil days. Lenox College at Hopkinton offers a striking example. Only a corporal's guard of students now attended, and most of the half-dozen ivy-clad brick buildings were occupied by the county high school, whose teachers in some cases taught in the college as well. Yet in the 1880's and 1890's Lenox had been the alma mater of the brothers John C. and Charles E. Merriam, who at this later period were respectively president of the Carnegie Institution in Washington and professor of political science at the University of Chicago.

As another device to bring the University closer to the state, the faculty every spring fanned out in all directions to deliver high-school commencement addresses. Although this cast me in an unfamiliar role, nothing could have acquainted me so well with the surroundings from which most of my students came. In one instance, indeed—the name of the place now forgotten—the graduating class consisted of but two members, a boy and a girl. They sat proudly on a platform in a basement room of the Methodist Church under a large, spreading banner inscribed LAUNCHED BUT NOT ANCHORED. The hall was packed, for it was a gala occasion for the entire vicinity, with the people paying a sort of admission fee by depositing gifts for the pair on a table at the door.

To supplement the policy of linking the University with the state, the History Department inaugurated on the campus an annual Conference of Teachers of History and the Social Studies. Professors from various Iowa colleges provided the papers along with our own staff, but the prime drawing card was always a distinguished figure, or more than one, from the Eastern seaboard. Among these were James Harvey Robinson and Carlton J. H. Hayes of Columbia, Charles M. Andrews and Max Farrand of Yale, and Albert Bushnell Hart of Harvard.

On other occasions historians of note came to deliver special lectures. Two from England stand out, though for opposite reasons. J. Holland Rose of Cambridge University at once won all our hearts by his gracious and genial personality. A. Percival

Newton of the University of London, on the other hand, was the traditional Briton at his worst—rude, supercilious, and self-centered. He obviously regarded himself a social lion, and it might have been said of him, as a Boston hostess had remarked many years before of a more eminent English scholar, E. A. Freeman, that he was in truth a king of beasts. At a dinner party Elizabeth and I gave for him he declined to shake hands with the guests, instructing them that this was not the English custom. Professor Andrews later told us that the only time in New Haven Newton appeared to realize he was not the sole person present was at the Harvard-Yale football game.

In a different category was Hamlin Garland, who remained for a few days after his talk. He had already written a number of novels and short stories about the frontier West and obviously enjoyed associating with professional historians. His autobiographical book *A Son of the Middle Border*, published several years before, had impressed me (and still does) as a minor American classic. Now he was engaged on a sequel to it, *A Daughter of the Middle Border*, and in due course he sent me an autographed copy. It seemed to me inferior to the earlier volume, and in a letter otherwise warmly appreciative I tactfully—or so I supposed—said as much. His reply made it evident he considered me a poor judge. I had yet to learn that an author's latest brain child is likely to be his best-loved one.

Meanwhile, as an outgrowth of the course on New Viewpoints in American History, I brought out a book under that title with Macmillan in April, 1922. The twelve essays treated such themes as "The Influence of Immigration on American History," "The Decline of Aristocracy in America," and "The Role of Women in American History," three of the chapters having previously appeared in learned journals in trial form. The volume was designed to direct the attention of the profession, and especially the younger members, to neglected or underemphasized aspects of the nation's development. Though four decades later it is all an old story, the book continues to sell a few hundred copies each year.

In preparation for writing it I had had perforce to read extensively in works off the beaten track, which also yielded ore for my course on Social and Cultural History. Even so, the need in a systematic class presentation to fill in the many gaps and pattern the data period by period constituted a formidable problem. I have never composed history lectures in which I learned so much in the process or afterward kept revising so drastically. If similar offerings were to become standard over the country, as I hoped, obviously the teachers must be provided with a ready-made body of subject matter. This, moreover, would suggest significant new lines of research. When a Macmillan representative showed up a month after *New Viewpoints* appeared, I accordingly proposed for the purpose the issuing of a multivolume co-operative *History of American Life*. The company at once seized on the idea, brought into the discussions Dixon Ryan Fox, now an associate professor at Columbia, and Carl Becker of Cornell, and in September I went to New York to help work out the details. A few months later, in February, 1923, Fox and I signed a contract to edit the undertaking, with Becker and, by subsequent agreement, Ashley H. Thorndike of Columbia in consulting capacities. Neither of us realized what a wolf we had grasped by the ears, that a project planned to end in three years would eventually require twenty-one. That summer and the next I spent with the family in Cambridge, Mass., collecting material at the Harvard and Boston libraries for my own volume in the series.

The Hawkeye state brought many new experiences, but perhaps the strangest was the political climate in which I found myself. Since Fremont ran for President in 1856 Iowa had gone Republican every time save 1912, when the party by dividing between Taft and Roosevelt enabled Wilson to carry the state.

And in this postwar era the leadership proved, if anything, more conservative than ever. Perhaps for this reason, my faculty friends by and large showed little interest in national questions, Herbert Goodrich being the principal exception. It was chiefly through reading the *New Republic* that it was possible to keep in touch with liberal currents of opinion.

As the 1920 election approached, I satisfied a long-felt curiosity to observe a nominating convention in action, and the Republicans by meeting in nearby Chicago determined my choice. No spectacle could have proved less edifying. For four days I sat through the baking June heat while party spellbinders ranted and raved, Senator Henry Cabot Lodge of Massachusetts capping them all with a poisonous personal attack on the now bedridden Wilson. Then, thanks to a midnight decision by an inner group in the famous "smoke-filled room"—of which we in the audience, of course, were ignorant—the nomination went on the tenth ballot to Warren G. Harding. So little known was the Ohio Senator that I overheard one of the spectators confidently identify him as the governor of Iowa, who bore the same surname. In the campaign the Republican candidate, it will be remembered, straddled and confused the crucial issue of League ratification, while his Democratic rival, James M. Cox, stoutly advocated America's joining. I unhesitatingly favored Cox, who, quite apart from his stand on the League, had earlier won my admiration by his progressive measures when three-term governor of Ohio. The fact that someone named Franklin D. Roosevelt shared the ticket made no impression on me one way or the other. In the sullen postwar mood of the country they, of course, stood no show.

When the election of 1924 came around, I again voted Democratic, but this time by absentee ballot, since I was then residing in Massachusetts, temporarily as I thought. John W. Davis, the party's standard-bearer, seemed to me clearly better qualified for the chief magistracy than the lethargic Calvin

Coolidge, who had inherited the White House mantle upon Harding's death. Senator La Follette, the nominee of the newborn Progressive party, made in some respects an even greater appeal, but my conviction as to the futility of third-party efforts removed him from consideration. The country, it need hardly be said, preferred to "Keep Cool with Coolidge."

Several weeks before the election I published in collaboration with Erik M. Eriksson, a graduate student who did the statistical work, an article in the *New Republic* entitled "The Vanishing Voter." It had no partisan implications but to my mind probed to the core the problem of popular government. It showed that from the presidential contest of 1856 through that of 1920 the ratio of actual to eligible voters had dropped from 83.5 per cent to a little more than 52—a fall of over a third despite the intervening spread of public education and better means of communication. The first of such inquiries, it may have helped to increase the number of nonpartisan get-out-the-vote campaigns in the years that followed.

Meanwhile I faithfully attended the American Historical Association, twice presenting papers. The Columbus gathering in December, 1923, offered more than the usual attractions. For one thing it took me back to old scenes and friends. For another, I had been asked to reply there to a Harvard invitation to become a visiting professor during the next academic year upon Frederick Jackson Turner's retirement from teaching. William S. Ferguson, the chairman of the History Department, had wired me some days before, and Turner and Channing had written warmly supporting letters. The salary was to be $6,000—$500 more than at Iowa—with an additional $500 for repeating one of my courses at Radcliffe College. The Department, unknown to me, was actually seeking a permanent replacement for Turner, but the tender looked merely like a stopgap arrangement until Samuel Eliot Morison, a Harvard product and colonial historian, should return after a year from his post as the first Harmsworth Professor of American History at Oxford University. Professor Archibald C. Coolidge and Frederick Merk, an instructor, conducted the negotiations. Upon learning that Merk would take over Turner's work in Western history and that I could give a lecture course and a seminar in social history, I accepted. The prospect of a year's residence in surroundings Elizabeth and I already knew and loved delighted both of us.

VI

Three Decades of Harvard

Cambridge in the mid-1920's was a sort of human palimpsest, its English colonial origins dimmed or erased by successive layers of population and the changes they effected until Irish Catholics had come to compose its most numerous element, as well as to man its factories and rule its politics. A favorite story told of the Hibernian conductor on the Massachusetts Avenue trolley line who at Linnaean Street, the stop for the Harvard Botanical Garden, cried out, "Linnehan Street." Probably in few places in America did town and gown maintain so little contact. Each looked at the other askance. The University community, though in the very midst of the city, lived almost exclusively to itself, jealously preserving its academic atmosphere and slower pace of life, and frequenting downtown Boston, ten minutes by subway, for its shopping and further cultural interests. It did not as yet possess a hotel or movie house, not even a five-and-ten-cent store. There were, of course, the usual shops for students, including a number of well-stocked secondhand bookstores, constantly replenished from the discarded libraries of old Cambridge families seeking smaller quarters. Thanks to these windfalls, I added precious items to my own collection. Brattle Street—the famous "Tory Row" of pre-Revolutionary days—constituted the finest residential section, retaining many of the old-time mansions with their well-tended grounds, while on the other side of the faculty district flowed the beautiful Charles River, dividing Cambridge from outlying Boston.

Harvard Yard—so named because the site had evolved in British times from a community cow yard—lay behind brick walls and counted among its buildings five of colonial vintage, in some of which General Washington had lodged soldiers during the siege of Boston. Dominating the scene was the monumental Widener Library, approached by a broad flight of steps leading to a row of massive Corinthian-capped columns at the entrance. Inside it was a scholar's paradise with a scholar in charge, the holdings arranged for the convenience of users rather than for that of the administrative staff, as is so generally the case. Fringing the Yard stood other buildings, erected wherever the authorities had been able to find space.

When I joined the faculty in the fall of 1924—for the time being, as I supposed—the major figures in European history were William S. Ferguson, Charles H. Haskins, Charles H. McIlwain, Archibald C. Coolidge, Roger B. Merriman, Wilbur C. Abbott, and Robert H. Lord, with Clarence H. Haring as the specialist on Latin America. In American history Edward Channing was the sole full professor, for the once famous trio of Channing, Hart, and Turner had been broken up, first by Hart's transferring some years before to the Government Department and now by Turner's retirement. Channing, however, taught only half time in order to make swifter progress with his *History of the United States,* thus putting the main burden of instruction on Frederick Merk, just promoted to assistant professor, and on me as a visitor. My program consisted of American Social and Intellectual History, a slight change in title but not in content from the Iowa offering; a related graduate seminar; the second half of the general course, of which

Merk gave the introductory portion; and a conference course for Seniors on Problems in the Diplomatic History of the United States. All but the first were a semester in length, and the two on social history were innovations.

I had been on the ground, however, but a short time when a bolt from the blue resulted in changing my status from temporary to permanent tenure. Columbia offered me a $6,000 professorship, to begin the next academic year. It was, in fact, James Harvey Robinson's long-occupied chair, now to be shifted to the American field. I went to New York to discuss the matter, conferring with Dixon Ryan Fox, Carlton J. H. Hayes, and others and ending the day with dinner at Hayes's apartment and an evening with him and his wife at the theater. On my return, while I was weighing my decision, though with little real doubt as to the outcome, word of the invitation leaked out at Harvard. At a football game the following Saturday I mentioned it to Merk in strictest secrecy, and Fred, for the only time in his life, I am sure, violated a confidence by reporting it to the senior members of the Department. On Monday came a matching offer from President Lowell.

What had seemed a fairly easy choice now became utter confusion. "How happy could I be with either, / Were t'other dear charmer away." I already knew Columbia from graduate days and greatly admired its historians. I would feel perfectly at home there. Insofar as the possibility of being called to a leading Eastern institution had ever occurred to me, I had thought only of Columbia. Harvard, on the other hand, was the nation's most ancient and, in many eyes, greatest seat of learning. The intellectual quality of both faculty and students had in the few weeks impressed me, and I would have a wholly free hand in developing social and cultural history. The fact, moreover, that it lay in a section of the country which had been a cradle of American liberty as well as of American literature exerted an influence. And, not least, Cambridge seemed a better place than Manhattan to raise a family.

Professor Turner, who returned that fall to deliver a series of public lectures, resolved my one remaining doubt. According to reports in the Middle West, his testy Yankee colleague Channing had made life so miserable for this son of a newer and rawer part of the United States that he had ever since regretted leaving Wisconsin. Understandably this gave me pause, since, if true, I could expect no different treatment. But Turner flatly and convincingly denied the tale and assured me that in my relations with Channing, as with all other colleagues, I would find Cambridge a congenial and stimulating environment. Meanwhile President Jessup came East with an offer to go back to Iowa at $500 above the Harvard-Columbia figure. Let me say at once that my choice of Harvard, where I was to spend the thirty years until retirement, turned out to be everything Turner had promised.

The appointment to a permanency necessitated a revision of domestic arrangements. Having taken for the year a furnished apartment, we brought on our household goods from Iowa City toward the end of this time and rented half of a double house while we looked for a place to buy. So much of the University neighborhood, however, dated from quite early days that otherwise attractive houses proved unsuitable because of their many rooms; some indeed lacked elementary conveniences. In one unforgettable case the daughter of a family having no electric lighting was engaged to a son of Thomas A. Edison, its famed inventor. Even in the fashionable Brattle Street district furnace heat did not always extend to all the rooms. In the end therefore we decided to build a home of our own. Fortunately, about a mile northwest of Harvard Square, land was available in a large estate which had recently come on the market and was being sold under zoning restrictions that ensured comfortable and pleasant dwellings. Gray Gardens, as the section was called, was named for Asa Gray, the nineteenth-century Harvard botanist, whose rambling frame house still stood nearby. Elizabeth drew up rough plans which an architect whipped into shape, and in the fall of 1926 we moved in. It was a brick house of colonial Georgian type, with large multipaned windows, a spacious living room with an open fireplace, and a third story under a sloping slate roof which accommodated a maid and a sixth bedroom. My study on the ground floor looked out on a deep garden which we enclosed on three sides with a high privet hedge and Elizabeth bordered with a flower bed. And at the rear was a garage for the automobile now acquired for the first time.

There our children spent their youth. Skeptical of any cut-and-dried formula for rearing them, we treated them from the earliest years in accordance with what seemed natural and sensible. They were expected to perform minor tasks about the house and yard in return for small allowances and, as they grew older, to assume increasing responsibility for their decisions and actions. Elizabeth, for instance, started them in at the Unitarian Sunday school and, to make attendance more attractive, taught a class herself for a time, but after a fair trial they chose to cease going. As a different example, each boy was given a dollar on the Fourth of July for fireworks and two dollars if he bought none, it being agreed that in any case they could shoot off harmless varieties like sparklers. This called for a critical—and probably unfair—weighing of values. Moreover, in practically every room of the house from top to bottom they were exposed to books, books, books, ranging from juvenile stories to standard literature, not to mention the scholarly works in my study; and these they were free to read at will. In like manner we always sought to respect their opinions and, if ill-founded, to meet them with reasoning. A Japanese youngster who dined with us was shocked at the free give-and-take at the table, observing that no parents in his country would have tolerated it.

As a matter of course the boys went to the Cambridge public schools. To Middle Westerners popular education was an article of faith, a necessary training ground in democratic ideas and associations. There was a good elementary school in the neighborhood; but we soon discovered that the schools in general were in a deplorable state, being staffed with ill-prepared teachers by an Irish-dominated and political-minded School Committee. For a number of years Elizabeth headed a group of the League of Women Voters to create public interest in bettering conditions, but with little effect. The fact was that by and large the "better" people were indifferent, having solved the problem by placing their own children in private schools. We remained firm, however, until Arthur's history teacher in the second year of high school told the pupils that the inhabitants of Albania were called Albinos because of their white hair and pink eyes. The next year we transferred him to Phillips Exeter Academy in New Hampshire, where the standards were unexceptionable. And when Tom finished the sixth grade he attended a private school in suburban Belmont. This sacrifice of principle did not come easily but appeared unavoidable if the boys were to have proper intellectual advantages.

In the summertime we usually rented a place for a month in the vicinity of Chatham, a small town at the elbow of Cape Cod. Motoring down through Quincy, the home of the historic Adams family, we would drive on to Plymouth, where the Pilgrims had landed; then, some miles beyond, cross the canal (which in fact converted the peninsula into an island) and follow winding woodland roads southeasterly for an hour to our cottage. There, on the sandy shore overlooking Nantucket Sound, with gulls making white arcs against the blue sky, the boys swam and played, hopefully chased skittering sandpipers and extended their knowledge of marine life, while the sun and wind tanned them to a nut brown. Between times, by foot and car we ranged all parts of the Cape, coming to love the low indented coastline, the lofty dunes, the pounding surf, the shiny inland ponds, the low-lying cranberry bogs, the trim little villages with white-spired churches. Many of the faculty vacationed in the mountains and woods of northern New England, but for us Cape Cod held an endless fascination.

Meanwhile the family of Xenia days continued to dwindle. Mother passed away in 1927 at the age of seventy-seven, and George in 1939 at fifty-five. He had for some years been executive director of the National Paving Brick Association in Washington, D.C. Of the original five children, now only Marion and I remained. Every year she visited us, and happily attained the age of eighty-six before she too died in 1962.

It proved slower to form close personal ties at Harvard than at Iowa. If life there had suggested that of a fishbowl, the Harvard community presented something of a cellular structure, with little communication among its parts. It was not that the faculty group was congenitally unsociable, but Cambridge was more than ten times larger than Iowa City and the professors jealously guarded their privacy for research and writing. Before long, however, I found myself on easy terms with Felix Frankfurter and his younger colleague James M. Landis, both of the Law School; and the three of us with our wives spent many evenings together in animated discussion. Then in my second year, when Reed Powell quit Columbia for the chair of constitutional law at Harvard, he and his wife joined the circle.

National and international events, state and University happenings, all ran the gantlet of the talk. Felix, but five feet five, more than compensated for his height with his exuberant spirits and vigor of expression. Generally the spark plug of the proceedings, he saucily interjected challenging comments for the evident purpose of provoking controversy. Then, he was a debater rather than a clarifier of issues, often gesticulating to underscore his points. But his steel-trap mind, informed by a knowledge of public affairs dating from his days as an assistant United States attorney in New York in 1906, always commanded attention if not always agreement. Jim, the least loquacious of the group, stuck in his oar when he thought it counted most, while Reed added his fillip of wit. In an argument over a constitutional question, for example, he quipped, "I naturally support the Constitution, because it supports me," though actually he delighted in attacking the Supreme Court's logic; and he once brought Felix up sharp by a reference to his "felixity of speech." Politically we all considered ourselves liberals except Powell, who, pluming himself on being above the battle, nevertheless usually wound up in the same camp.

Frankfurter, ordinarily no respecter of persons—President Lowell was a favorite target—placed one individual on an unassailable pedestal. This was Justice Oliver Wendell Holmes, a long-time friend, whose mind and judicial opinions he admired beyond compare. When I mentioned casually one night that Professor Richard C. Cabot, another old friend of Holmes, considered the Justice a vain man, Felix erupted like a sky-rocket and devoted the rest of the evening to upbraiding me for repeating the remark and Cabot for ever making it. With some difficulty I gathered he was not so much interested in rebutting the description as in contending—unfairly so far as Cabot was concerned—that a prophet hath honor save in his own country, the country in this instance being, of course, that of provincial-minded and effete Brahmins. Nor was he deterred when his hitherto silent wife, upon my asking, agreed with Cabot. Still fuming as we split up, Felix wrote me a few days later reiterating his sentiments and again flaying Boston's "arid" and "conventional intellectual climate."

Our little group suffered its first loss when Landis departed for Washington in 1933 to join the Federal Trade Commission as a New Deal appointee, and an irreparable one when Frankfurter in 1939 was named to the Supreme Court. In that august body, until he retired nearly a quarter of a century later, he was stoutly to champion the constitutional principles for which he had so revered Holmes.

Among other colleagues I early came to prize were Ralph

Barton Perry of the Philosophy Department and Edwin F. Gay in Economics. Perry, a quiet, friendly man who avoided professional jargon outside the classroom, had a strong interest in public affairs, which he viewed pretty much as I did. Gay, more conservative in outlook, combined wartime experience in government with an exhaustive knowledge of economic history and brought a hardheaded judgment to the discussion of political questions. And half inside and half outside the Harvard family was another companion, Bernard De Voto— "Benny" to his friends—a novelist and nationally known literary critic who taught for some years in the English Department, then stayed on in Cambridge as a free-lance writer. Combative in utterance, a hater of sham in every form, Benny wished above all else to attain professional recognition as a historian of the Far West and did indeed win the Pulitzer Prize with one of his books. A still wider cross-section of the faculty I came to know through the so-called Shop Club. The thirty or forty members, chosen from a variety of disciplines, dined together monthly and heard and discussed papers setting forth their particular research interests. This introduced me to areas of knowledge, especially in the scientific field, which had before been a closed book.

On the purely social side, the almost universal attitude toward national prohibition stood in bald contrast to that at Iowa and came, I confess, as something of a shock. Despite my German upbringing the Eighteenth Amendment had on balance seemed a wise provision. It had been adopted after a century of agitation and experiment and, besides, promised to end the evil influence of the liquor interests in politics. Moreover, the action, having been ratified by nine more than the required number of states—only three holding out— appeared to pose no serious difficulties of enforcement. Sadly misreading the omens, I did not foresee the rise of the illicit traffic, or that the first President in office after its adoption would himself flout it, and that private citizens normally law-abiding would freely reject what to them was an unwarranted invasion of their privacy. Nearly everywhere Elizabeth and I were invited our hosts served drinks, and rather than give offense we found ourselves imbibing, even though we scrupulously furnished none to our own guests. But we could not long justify the dual standard, so when Benny De Voto, about to motor across the Canadian border to replenish his own supply, offered to obtain some for us, we too succumbed. We felt red-faced, though, when young Tom, seeing the bottles, inquired of his mother, "Is Daddy a bootlegger?" Not till the amendment's repeal in 1933 made social drinking legal again did our consciences really rest easy.

Rapport with my history colleagues came about naturally, not only because of a common concern with the past but because of the weekly luncheons at which everyone freely aired his views on departmental matters. Although Professor Channing, working against time to finish the concluding two volumes of his *History of the United States,* never attended, his office and mine lay nearby in the Widener stacks, and I saw him almost daily. He had graduated from Harvard ten years before I was born and under his gruff exterior regarded me with a paternal eye. Once, indeed, when he thought my desk poorly lighted, he installed his own floor lamp until I purchased one like it. Though delighting to deride the "crude" Middle West, he expected retorts in kind, which he never failed to get. When he (rightly, of course) jeered at the demagoguery of Mayor Thompson of Chicago, I blandly observed he had evidently forgotten that "Big Bill" was a native of Boston, and wondered why that center of culture turned to the Chicago Civic Company for its annual season of grand opera. Again, when he reproached me for supporting the New Yorker Al Smith for President in 1928, it was, I explained, because he had at last convinced me of the superiority of any Easterner over any Westerner, only now to find him backing Herbert Hoover, a Californian born in Iowa.

Channing died in January, 1931, of a cerebral hemorrhage at the age of seventy-five, leaving behind the manuscript of the seventh and last volume of his *History*. During the hour of the funeral all classes were suspended, a tribute accorded no one else during my connection with Harvard. A few weeks later his widow asked me what she should do with the work, and unhappily, after a careful reading, I was obliged to advise her not to publish it, for even with skillful editing it could add nothing to his reputation and might well diminish it. The fact was that in moving beyond the oft-trodden ground of the period before 1865 Channing had shown little grasp of the new forces of industrialization and urbanization which in the century's final years transformed the country. Mrs. Channing, to my profound relief, evidenced no surprise, quietly remarking that she herself had observed a falling off of Edward's mental faculties. The outcome undoubtedly would have been far different had Channing essayed the volume at the peak of his powers.

The two full-time American historians other than myself, Merk in Western history and Morison in the colonial field, were approximately my age. Fred, a quiet unassuming man of Wisconsin birth, lean and wiry in build, roomed with us for some years until his marriage in 1931, before which time he had acquired permanent tenure. In and out of the house we discussed historical problems, which his keen analytical mind always illuminated. He was a Turnerian, of course, but in no slavish sense. As a student and friend of the master he knew that Turner himself, unlike some of his disciples, eschewed dogmatism. He was one of the ablest teachers in the Department but, again like Turner, was so much of a perfectionist as to be slow to confide the results of his researches to print.

Sam Morison, who arrived in my second year, after his stint at Oxford, resembled an old-time Puritan worthy in austerity of mien, though not in interests and tastes. Tall and spare, he lived on Beacon Hill in Boston in the house in which he was

born and was one of the very few to my knowledge who spoke
with what is termed elsewhere the "Harvard accent." An unusually gifted writer, he was also an extremely prolific one.
His love of salt water led him to unite scholarship with
pleasure in such works as *Admiral of the Ocean Sea* and—
quite outside the colonial era—the multivolume *History of
United States Naval Operations in World War II*. Severe in
his judgments of people, Sam did not suffer fools gladly, and
in that category he placed students who confused industry
with intelligence. He cavalierly dropped his Radcliffe teaching,
for instance, when he found girls copying into their notebooks
his jocose as well as his serious observations. Our own relations were invariably cordial. Among his many other kind-
nesses he saw that I was early elected to the Massachusetts
Historical Society, the American Antiquarian Society, and the
Colonial Society of Massachusetts, and this brought me in
touch with the abler lay historians of the region.

Thanks to the stiffer entrance requirements, high tuition,
and restricted enrollment, the undergraduates by and large
came from more literate homes than at the two state universities where I had taught. Prior to President Lowell's accession
in 1909, "C" had been held "the gentleman's grade," but his
introduction of the tutorial system radically changed this. This
more personalized form of instruction supplemented classroom courses in the student's chosen field, enabling him to
fill in the gaps and relate the whole to an intellectual setting
involving allied branches of knowledge. Now he typically
strove to do his best, and a very large proportion achieved
honors. Football, for example, did not submerge all other interests in the autumn; even a defeat by Yale, Harvard's traditional rival, caused only fleeting disappointment. And, by the
same token, the faculty placed an emphasis on first-rate teaching beyond anything I had known. Senior members did not
regard it beneath their dignity to offer introductory courses,
contrary to the usual practice of entrusting this important

function to novices. Consequently I too now devoted more thought than ever before to my lectures.

Lowell effected a further revolution in the student body with the so-called House plan. By clustering all undergraduates except Freshmen in groups of a few hundred in residential units, each with its common room, library, dining and recreational facilities, he re-established some of the flavor and friendliness of a small college; and by attaching faculty members to the units he narrowed the distance between teachers and taught. As an Associate of Adams House I observed the resulting social and intellectual advantages; and Arthur, who lived there in his three upper years after finishing at Exeter, experienced them at first hand. The once strong influence exerted by the old exclusive clubs on student life now declined almost to the vanishing point.

After the first two years I dropped the class for Seniors on American diplomatic problems and gave full time from then on to my part of the general course and to social and intellectual history. The general course contained around 225 students except in the aftermath of World War II, when the flood of returning G.I.'s temporarily swelled the number to nearly 700. The lectures treated the subject matter interpretatively, leaving the factual details to the textbook—of which more will be said in the next chapter—and the members also did extensive supplementary reading, for which they were held strictly accountable in examinations. The course on social and intellectual history usually drew from 75 to 100, divided about equally between advanced undergraduate and graduate students. Here, because of the novelty of the material, the lectures carried the principal burden; the class, in addition to enlarging their knowledge by outside reading, prepared papers on special topics. Some of the reports proved of such merit as to be subsequently published. One graduate student, now teaching in a large Eastern university, called the course "a seedbed of doctoral theses." There, indeed, he came across the subject he himself wrote on.

A much richer seedbed, however, was the allied seminar which, limited to ten or a dozen doctoral candidates, concerned itself specifically with the training of future historians. To secure them at a formative stage the offering fell in the first semester. After discussing past conceptions and directions of American historiography I focused on the main aims of the course. These were to expound historical method, direct attention to the wealth of bibliographical and other tools of the trade, impart the approved ways of scholarly citation, and —the crowning feature—induct the students into original investigation on their own. They first presented their results orally for group criticism and then in writing for my approval. Many of these papers also appeared later in journals. Doubtless these procedures were much the same in other graduate centers, but they differed greatly from the somewhat hit-and-miss, sink-or-swim practices in the Columbia of my day. There, to mention a single aspect, considerations of literary form went unnoticed; it sufficed if the findings were somehow made intelligible. Without expecting to turn out belletrists I constantly bore down on Benjamin Franklin's dictum that the exposition "be *smooth, clear,* and *short,*" elements of style which, having presumably been learned in Freshman composition courses, had a way of being forgotten. One of my great satisfactions was to see individuals who had been made conscious of their deficiencies afterward become effective writers of doctoral theses.

The students nearly always responded eagerly to the training, accepting its rigors as a price of entering the profession. Of the few exceptions to the rule the most unusual perhaps was the naval reserve officer of old New England stock who, reporting on "The Social Ideas of Mark Twain," announced some decidedly bizarre conclusions. When asked for his documentary evidence, he bridled and challenged me instead to attend a séance of his spiritualist where he would query Mark himself. This indeed was a short cut to historical verity which could save scholars untold hours of laborious research, and I silently wondered whether its proponent could be an unreconstructed descendant of the Salem believers in witches. I expressed willingness provided, however, the medium would first reveal the location of the body of a New York stockbroker whose death in the Maine woods was just then making newspaper headlines. Indignant at this show of skepticism, he disappeared thereafter from the seminar.

Every Sunday afternoon Elizabeth and I kept open house to graduate students. Having done this occasionally at Iowa, we now made it a regular practice. Seated before the blazing log fire in winter or out in the garden when spring arrived, the company would discuss, if not shoes and ships and sealing wax, then just about everything else under the sun. The spirited exchanges brought young and old together in an informal and relaxed relationship. As in the miracle of the loaves and the fishes, Elizabeth magically produced tea, and sandwiches and brownies, whether the callers were few or many. In the preface to his doctoral thesis *The Circuit Rider Dismounts* (1938) Hunter D. Farish said he spoke for himself as well as "a host of other history students" in expressing gratitude for "the oases in our work provided by her gracious hospitality." But this was only one side of the story. For us, too, it was a continuing source of pleasure and made me, I am sure, a better teacher.

As social and intellectual history represented my special interest and teemed with subjects crying for investigation, it is hardly surprising that the theses under my direction fell almost exclusively in that area. They numbered sixty-four in the thirty years, with three others at Radcliffe. Once a student settled on a theme, he went on his own way until he had accumulated enough data to distinguish the forest from the trees and submit a tentative outline. This might require some months if he could devote full time to the project, or several years if he meanwhile took up teaching duties. Then when he began writing I scrutinized his work chapter by chapter from the triple standpoint of exhaustiveness of research, soundness of reasoning, and language. In the long run this economized time for each of us. The following comment offered in a letter years afterward represents one reaction to the procedure:

Vivid recollections still remain with me of the first couple of chapters I sent you, and the shape they were in when you sent them back. I was thoroughly discouraged then, but time has since proved to me that just that exceedingly careful and detailed criticism is the exactly unique feature of the graduate education I received at Harvard.

The afterthoughts of others were, I trust, little different. More than any honorary degrees, I have treasured the nine dedications of books to me by former students.

It was my happy lot to attract exceedingly able ones. Professor John Higham, not himself of Harvard, wrote in the *American Historical Review* in 1951 that they comprised "a sizable share of the best Ph.D.'s in United States history" and that cumulatively they had made probably "the most impressive contribution" in the social and intellectual field. Two of the number (Merle Curti and Carl Bridenbaugh) later became presidents of the American Historical Association, and others presidents of the Mississippi Valley Historical Association and the Southern Historical Association. As for special laurels accorded theses, one (Paul H. Buck) received a Pulitzer Prize; four (Bridenbaugh, Richard W. Leopold, Oscar Handlin, and Donald H. Fleming), American Historical Association awards; and two (Ira V. Brown and Timothy L. Smith), comparable recognition by the American Society of Church History. Moreover, two (Curti and Handlin) won Pulitzer Prizes for subsequent writings. Buck, Handlin, and Fleming are now full professors at Harvard, and if it is proper to include my son

Arthur, he too was one for some years. Arthur, however, never enrolled for a doctorate, obtaining equivalent training as a member of Harvard's Society of Fellows, a postgraduate berth which enabled him to spend three years on research of his own. *The Age of Jackson* (1945), which resulted, also earned a Pulitzer award.

Midway in my fourth year, at the start of 1928, I became chairman of the Department, a post I did not seek or want but which rotated among the senior professors. I accepted on condition that the term be minimal and that a half-time secretary assist with the letters and records. It is hard to realize in the Harvard of today that the custom then was to carry on the correspondence through an overburdened central typing bureau. The duties of the office were purely administrative, for the major decisions were made jointly by the permanent members, and the minor ones by the entire staff at the weekly luncheons. The only untoward incident occurred when with the dean's and the Department's approval I cabled Gaetano Salvemini in London asking him to teach for a semester. The internationally known historian, long a professor at the University of Florence, had fled his native Italy to escape Fascist oppression. Before he answered, however, President Lowell notified me that an influential member of the Corporation (Harvard's highest governing body) strongly objected to the invitation and that it must be rescinded while time still permitted. This was the period, now painful to remember, when many well-intentioned Americans hailed Mussolini as his country's benefactor, the leader who had succeeded in imposing needed discipline on a disorderly people. To such persons a Salvemini was a troublemaker and a radical. I replied that since we had acted with proper authorization the offer could not in honor be withdrawn. Lowell may himself have had doubts about the proceeding. In any event he did not pursue the matter further.

Salvemini made such a fine impression on us that after James

B. Conant became president in 1933 the Department in due course secured him on a regular basis. A warm, colorful, vital personality, he won a distinctive place in the entire University community. Broad-shouldered and rotund, he conversed with his whole body, waving his arms and grimacing, and his ready wit and thickly accented pronunciation added to the effect. For instance, at a meeting of the Shop Club, which early elected him, he exclaimed in an audible whisper while listening to a talk on the School of Education, "Eet eess a factory of fog!"; and the chuckles that ran round the room indicated that others wished they could have said it as concisely. Beyond his academic duties he maintained constant relations with Italo-American groups in Boston and New York to expose, as only he could, the beguilements of Fascist propaganda in the United States.

In the meantime my release had come about from the chairmanship—or "choremanship," as it was sometimes not unaptly called—thanks to an unexpected development. In January, 1930, Robert M. Hutchins, the new president of the University of Chicago, offered me a professorship at $12,000—half again as much as at Harvard—with freedom to teach whatever I wanted or not at all. Hutchins's action was part of a campaign to raid other institutions after the fashion of William Rainey Harper, who in the 1890's had assembled Chicago's original faculty. The prospect of devoting all the time I wished to research and writing attracted me to the extent of visiting Chicago to discuss the matter, but the policy of paying newcomers at higher figures than equally good or better professors on the ground gave me pause. It may be that in any case I would have stayed at Harvard, for I had come to feel it was my spiritual home. The dean, however, made the decision easy. He not only engaged to relieve me of the chairmanship, but to keep me abreast of every new advance in the salary scale and grant me the departmental secretary for my personal use. This last arrangement enabled me to utilize the services of Elizabeth F. Hoxie, a Wellesley graduate, who, besides being an accomplished typist, has through the years assisted me also in my scholarly work.

Apart from this tour of administrative duty I served on a good many committees. Among those particularly interesting were the Administrative Board of the Graduate School, the Committee on the University Library, the Committee on Higher Degrees in American Civilization as well as the Committee on the History of Science and Learning. Another, the Phillips Brooks House Committee, overlooked students engaged in voluntary social work in the Greater Boston community. Besides these permanent boards, a special Committee on the Objectives of a General Education in a Free Society reorganized the undergraduate curriculum in line with President Conant's directive to supplement specialized knowledge with "some continuing contact with those fields in which value judgments are of prime importance." The resulting report, published in 1945, sold 50,000 copies in the next decade, an indication of the nationwide attention it excited.

Still another assignment deserves somewhat extended notice because the circumstances were unique in Harvard history. In Conant's early years, before he mastered his job, a storm blew up among the younger faculty over his refusal to renew the three-year appointments, unanimously recommended by the Economics Department, of two instructors, J. Raymond Walsh and Alan R. Sweezy. The suspicion or conviction obtained that the decision stemmed not from an evaluation of the men's teaching and scholarship but from a dislike of their unorthodox social and economic views. Both had taken an active interest in the Massachusetts labor movement and been leaders in the Harvard Teachers' Union, an affiliate of the American Federation of Labor. On May 3, 1937, one hundred and forty-one members of the junior staff sent a fifteen-page printed *Memorandum* to nine full professors, of whom I was one, expressing "misgivings" at the action and asking that these "academic seniors . . . tell us after all necessary inquiry whether they are without foundation." The signers included such men of later note on the faculty as Crane Brinton, Paul H. Buck, Sterling Dow, Rupert Emerson, Merle Fainsod, John K. Fairbank, J. Kenneth Galbraith, Wilbur K. Jordan, Talcott Parsons, Walter Piston, Willard V. Quine, and E. Bright Wilson, Jr. Few departments of learning were un-represented.

We who were so addressed found ourselves in an unenviable position. We had no desire to head a domestic insurrection but, on the other hand, believed that so large a body of peti-tioners had every right to have their concern responsibly probed. Behind the specific grievance, however, as we well knew, lay a more basic problem. In the booming 1920's the Lowell regime had been able to expand the faculty at will, for additional funds were always obtainable; but with the coming of the Great Depression and a relatively unchanging budget the Conant administration was confronted with the need to exercise the utmost foresight in making promotions and ap-pointments. The authorities, though, had given little heed to the necessity, so that hiring and firing in the junior ranks sometimes bore the aspect of offhand judgments, causing men at this level to feel that their worth was not duly weighed. This underlying condition, we believed, helped explain the un-paralleled explosion over the fate of the two economics in-structors. We determined therefore to make this wider situation an essential phase of our inquiry. Wishing if possible not to work at odds with the administration, we placed the circumstances of our appointment before Conant, who promptly named us his own committee with full access to the facilities and records of his office. This evidenced that ab-sence of self-pride—that willingness always to reconsider a de-cision—which characterized his make-up. It is hard to think of Lowell ever so acting.

The Committee of Eight—one of the original number died

before we had proceeded very far—consisted, besides myself, of Ralph Barton Perry (chairman), William S. Ferguson
in Greek history, Kenneth B. Murdock in English, Harlow
Shapley in astronomy, and three law professors: E. Merrick
Dodd, Jr., Felix Frankfurter, and Edmund M. Morgan. Tackling first the Walsh-Sweezy case, we met weekly during term
time, taking oral and written testimony, and in May, 1938,
submitted our conclusions in eighty-six printed pages. We ab-
solved the administration of political or economic bias, declaring that "there was no departure whatsoever from Harvard's
tradition of tolerance and untrammelled inquiry," but nevertheless recommended the reinstatement of the two men on the
ground that their merits had not received fair consideration.
The President and the Corporation somewhat bluntly rejected
the recommendation, but urged us to go ahead with the second part of the investigation, the broader problem of criteria
of appointments, reappointments, promotions, and tenure.

So, with heads bloody but unbowed, we accordingly proceeded in the autumn. To tap as diversified sources of information as possible, we not only consulted with departmental chairmen but obtained the views in writing of 201 of
the younger teachers. Again we held weekly meetings, with additional sessions in the final stages. There is no need here to
particularize our findings, which were set forth in a published
report of 165 pages in March, 1939. Suffice it to say that they
completely revolutionized the system of faculty recruitment,
advancement, and tenure, including the introduction of a
new and more logical salary scale. This time Conant expressed
"keen satisfaction," the faculty enthusiastically approved the
proposals, and the president appointed Ferguson of our
committee to the deanship of Arts and Sciences to put the
regulations into effect.

Two other accomplishments of the Conant regime also enlisted my warm interest, and in these, unlike the case of the
Committee of Eight, he was the prime mover. One was the

forging of a more integral relationship with Radcliffe. Since its founding in 1879 that college had had to get along with such undergraduate instruction as members of the Harvard faculty, teaching for additional pay, were willing to offer, the diplomas then being signed by the heads of the two institutions. Lowell heartily disliked the connection and kept President Ada L. Comstock on tenterhooks lest it be severed and Radcliffe cast adrift. Conant, on the contrary, entered into an arrangement in 1943 which opened all Harvard courses to the girls in return for a lion's share of Radcliffe's tuition fees. Thenceforth the two sexes stood on equal plane, attending the same classes. "Harvard," Conant dryly remarked (or so it was reported), "does not believe in coeducation in principle —only in practice." Surprisingly enough, the expected clamor from outraged Harvard alumni failed to materialize.

In both eras I taught Radcliffe students, and in 1942 became a member of its governing board, the Council, which occupied a position comparable to that of the Corporation at Harvard. And a year later, when Miss Comstock retired, I served on the special committee which chose as her successor Wilbur K. Jordan, then a professor of English history at the University of Chicago. In his nearly seventeen years he added greatly to the institution's laurels, one of his many innovations being the establishment of a Women's Archives as a national center for research into their contributions in all spheres of American thought and action. Since this promised to close one of the gaps in historical writing noted in *New Viewpoints*, I gladly acted as chairman of its Advisory Board for more than a decade. It was this body which recommended the publication by Radcliffe of a biographical cyclopedia of outstanding members of the sex in the past. That undertaking, to be entitled *Notable American Women,* has for several years been in course of preparation under the editorship of Edward T. James, one of my Ph.D.'s.

The other project of Conant's close to my heart was the Nieman Foundation, the outgrowth of a bequest to the University for elevating the standards of journalism, which he used to give unusually promising newspaper men and women a year of self-directed study at Harvard in subjects calculated to enrich their background. For some years I served on the selection committee, traveling to various parts of the country to interview candidates. A special feature of the plan was the monthly dinners at which well-known columnists, foreign correspondents, editors, and publishers spoke, with a sprinkling of faculty guests to join in the lively discussions which always ensued. In addition, Louis M. Lyons, the quietly effective director and himself a former journalist, edited a quarterly magazine, *Nieman Reports,* which assessed the performance and failings of the press. After retiring from the faculty I dedicated a book, *Prelude to Independence,* to "The Nieman Fellows of Harvard University, Past and Present," and Lyons's comment on this in the *Nieman Reports* will sufficiently suggest the nature of my participation in the enterprise. Schlesinger, he said,

has been a friend to all of them from the beginning. He has often said that he placed his activity for the Nieman Foundation second only to his profession of history. He . . . regularly attended the gatherings of the Nieman Fellows. Each Fall at the opening, for many years, he has scheduled a day to sit at the Nieman office and hold individual consultations with each incoming Fellow, to advise him on his plans for study. The personal relationships thus begun have carried down the years and across the land.

Of my thirty years at Harvard, nine were under Lowell, twenty under Conant, and the final one under Nathan M. Pusey, who took over in 1953. In this span of time I formed certain abiding impressions of the institution and its place in the intellectual world. To begin with, it was, as already noted, not only a community of scholars but also of teachers, both functions being deemed vital to the advancement and diffusion of knowledge. Nor did this oldest of American universities, as might be expected, suffer from debilities of age. It almost seemed on occasion that nothing was permanent but change, that the long acceptance of an educational theory or practice, instead of hallowing it, constituted a reason for trying something else. There was an unceasing spirit of revolt against repose. The Tercentenary celebration in 1936, attended by a host of scholars from all over the globe, proved a time more of looking forward than backward, of doing honor, as one speaker said, to a seat of learning "disciplined but not fettered by the past." Of Lowell's more important reforms there have been mentioned in passing the tutorial system, the House plan, and the Society of Fellows, and, of Conant's, the program of general education, the new basis of faculty appointments and tenure, the closer link with Radcliffe, and the Nieman undertaking. Incidentally, both men, too, contributed to the brick-and-mortar expansion of the University until the Yard as I first knew it lost much of its old-time character, with many additional buildings populating the environs.

Intellectual diversity flowered naturally in a soil fertilized by minds from all parts of the country and the world. Faculty inbreeding—"academic incest," in Reed Powell's pungent term —was in disrepute except, oddly enough, at the very highest administrative level, where in the persons of Lowell and Conant, and before them of Charles W. Eliot, the selection of Harvard College alumni to the presidency had produced educational statesmen of nationwide influence. In this onetime Yankee stronghold Morison, for instance, was the only full-time American historian with a Harvard A.B., Merk as well as I being state-university graduates from that far-off clime which Channing called Transappalachia; and presently we were joined by another Midwesterner, similarly educated, Paul Buck, whom Conant in due course made provost of the University. And others in the Department hailed from Canada, England, Italy, and Russia.

Harvard, moreover, evinced constant awareness of belong-

ing to the greater society of the state and nation, an attitude
going back to colonial days and resulting in graduates serving
at every level of the government. President Franklin D.
Roosevelt, class of 1904, who took time off from pressing duties to participate in the Tercentenary, was a symbol of this
enduring spirit. Few, incidentally, will forget seeing him at
one of the outdoor sessions seated with bare head during a
sudden downpour of rain and disdaining an umbrella. In the
same tradition of public service members of the faculty stood
ready at a moment's notice to contribute their special talents
in peace and war.

I had expected Harvard to be a citadel of academic freedom, and so it proved. Conant's declaration in the *Atlantic
Monthly* in 1935 that "We must have our share of thoughtful
rebels," and that the "clash of opinion" necessarily enters into
the social sciences and humanities, spoke for Lowell as well
as for himself. Neither wished the institution to turn out a
standardized product with uniform ideas of life and society;
that would defeat the very purpose of a liberal education. A
test came late in 1939 when a student organization, the Young
Communist League, engaged Earl Browder, general secretary
of the American Communist party, for an address. No difficulty would have arisen but for the fact that, before the time
for the talk arrived, a federal grand jury in New York indicted
Browder for violation of passport regulations, and the officer
in University Hall charged with assigning rooms for meetings
thereupon withdrew his consent. On its face this looked like
an infringement of the principle of freedom of learning inasmuch as it prejudged the outcome of a case which a petit jury
had yet to determine. Accordingly, Arthur N. Holcombe of
the Government Department, Kirtley Mather in geology,
David W. Prall in philosophy, and I protested the action to
the Corporation on the ground that under Anglo-American
law a man is deemed innocent until proven guilty. The members, though disappointing us by failing to overrule their ad-

ministrative functionary, otherwise rose to the occasion to our full satisfaction. They roundly affirmed, "The policy of Harvard has for a long time been to favor free expression within wide limits and not to restrict or interfere with such expression, however unorthodox, controversial or unpopular," adding, "This policy should and will be continued." To that end they provided that all future questions involving the fitness of a speaker should be decided by a committee composed of three members of the faculty and three of the Student Council, with myself as chairman. Harvard thus issued from the episode stronger in its stand, if possible, than earlier. No need ever arose, even under the emotional stresses of World War II, for the committee to be called together.

VII

Other Professional Activities

Professorial duties aside, my time went into talks of a historical character away from Cambridge and into research and writing, with a bizarre intrusion projecting me temporarily into a distant municipal election because of a previously published book. Of the speaking engagements, one of the first was in the nature of a sentimental journey—to give the commencement address at Ohio State in 1926—which took Elizabeth and me back to our early days together as well as to familiar sights and friends. The discourse itself afforded an opportunity to decry the spirit of intellectual and social conformity which infected the country following World War I.

Under the title "The New Tyranny" I depicted the factors which in the century and a half since the Declaration of Independence had produced periodical waves of intolerance, such as that currently evidenced by the reborn Ku Klux Klan, the would-be censorship of history schoolbooks, and the legislative bans on the teaching of biological evolution. Unless these forces of repression were dispelled, as they had been by earlier generations, the nation, I said, would lose "those sources of fresh inspiration, and of those new alternatives to old ways of doing things, which form the very breath of life in a progressive society." Naturally the press featured the passage:

The typical American today may be pictured as a man wearing a Knox hat, an Arrow collar, a Manhattan shirt, a Hart, Schaffner and Marx suit, and a pair of Walk-Over shoes, seated in a Ford car with a *Saturday Evening Post* under his arm on his way to the monthly meeting of the National Association for the Banishment of Privacy from the American Home.

On the institutions of higher learning, I concluded, lay the primary obligation to ensure freedom of thought and conduct, but to accomplish this they must radically reform many present educational methods. The speech could hardly have pleased an Ohio audience which in this heyday of Coolidge prosperity rejoiced in what they believed to be the best of all possible worlds. However, the only adverse comments repeated to me concerned my condemnation of peacetime military drill at the University, which, by demanding unquestioning obedience, contravened the academic ideal of "cultivating individual initiative, independent thinking, and intellectual leadership."

In berating the assaults on American history teaching I had no premonition of myself becoming one of the targets. To understand how this came about one must recall the mood of the country after "Mr. Wilson's war." In the widespread revulsion to "foreign entanglements" a potent ingredient was the conviction that Britain had tricked us into the struggle, thus unmasking herself as still the ancient enemy of 1776. And the reason she had succeeded, it was charged, lay in the schoolbooks which, once ardently patriotic, now vitiated their treatment of pre-Revolutionary events by presenting also the English side of the story. At the van of the offensive stood such virtuous organizations as the Sons and the Daughters of the American Revolution, the Descendants of the Signers of the Declaration of Independence, the Grand Army of the

Republic, the American Legion, and the Veterans of Foreign Wars. Some of them went so far as to charge eminent historians with doctoring their texts for British gold and plotting "to bring the United States back into the British Empire." Official investigations of "Anglicized" books occurred in New York City, Washington, D.C., St. Louis, and elsewhere, and at least three states, Wisconsin, Oklahoma, and Oregon, enacted "pure history" laws. In a write-up of the hysteria for the *Publishers' Weekly* I closed on the note:

Those persons who wish to perpetuate a false picture of the past, who want everything but the hurrahs left out of the history books, pride themselves upon being patriots. On the contrary, they are men of little faith who deep down in their hearts suspect that our country's history contains things so discreditable that it is not well for young ears to hear them.

The frenzy assumed its grossest form in Chicago, where William Hale Thompson, running for mayor in the spring of 1927, seized on the agitation for political advantage. Backed by the violently isolationist Chicago *Tribune,* he won the office through artfully exploiting the Anglophobe prejudices of immigrant groups and promising to "biff King George on the snoot" should he ever come there. Quite innocently I became involved because *New Viewpoints in American History,* published five years earlier, was on the reading list of a course for teachers at the University of Chicago and, according to Representative John J. Gorman of Chicago in the *Congressional Record,* March 9, 1927, the work teemed with "unAmerican and unpatriotic statements," referring to George Washington as "a great disloyalist and rebel" and casting "corresponding aspersions" on other revered leaders. "Big Bill," for his part, brandished the "infamous book" at his rallies and pledged he would "stop the defamation of America's heroes" as well as see that justice was done to "the heroes of Irish, Polish, German, Holland, Italian and other extractions."

Coming to my defense, Rupert Hughes, a recent biographer of Washington, retorted in the magazine *Current History,* "Mayor Thompson quotes with animus only so much as he wants to quote." I myself did not enter the fray, being willing to let the book speak for itself. *New Viewpoints,* in fact, devoted an entire and highly appreciative chapter to "The Influence of Immigration on American History," while the alleged denigration of Washington appeared in a single sentence introducing the essay on "The American Revolution," a sentence, one would suppose, difficult for any literate person to misunderstand:

When the representatives of George V rendered homage a few years ago at the tomb of the great disloyalist and rebel of a former century, George Washington, the minds of many Americans reverted, with a sense of bewilderment, to the times when another King George was guiding the destinies of the British nation.

Yet even after the election "Big Bill" for a time kept up the din. At his behest, for example, "Sport" Herrmann, one of his staff, endeavored to remove the "treason-tainted" volume from the public library and, upon failing, bought a copy which he then burned publicly as a "symbolic" act. Friends congratulated me on the free advertising, and had the "new viewpoints" concerned sex, no doubt the sales might have benefited. As it was, they showed no effects either good or bad.

Although the criticism of history texts presently subsided—in Chicago as elsewhere—a somewhat similar if less extensive wave of distrust arose in the mid-1930's, prompted this time by fear that European history books were Communist-slanted. Even Cornell's Carl Becker, perhaps the most thoughtful defender of democratic principles and basic human rights in the entire historical guild, came under fire because of his popular high-school textbook *Modern History.* The storm centered in the District of Columbia, where a citizens' group in November, 1935, charged him with "advocating the Russian Soviet system." Becker responded by inviting a number of his academic friends to wire the president of the Board of Education "whether I am a communist and whether my books advocate communism." His letter of thanks for my own telegram made clear the real nature of his concern:

Of course I don't personally give a damn what these nit-wits think of me, but the school authorities and teachers need what help they can be given in their fight for decent conditions of teaching in the schools. The telegrams are helping a good bit, & the indications now are that the effort to exclude my book will fail. The real fight appears to be a political one—an effort to get Ballou, Supt. of Schools, out in order to give his job to a Democrat.

Becker read the portents right, but not all the other authors under attack fared so well.

Of my articles five may be worth recalling as suggesting fresh avenues for scholarly inquiry. "Social History in American Literature," published in the *Yale Review*, 1928 (and later that year in *The Reinterpretation of American Literature*, edited by Norman Foerster), argued the need for studying literature as a direct or indirect expression of social and economic conditions rather than as something which had developed "in a vacuum, without relation to anything but itself"; and the essay further urged that the researches extend beyond belles-lettres to the reading matter of the masses, which in a democratic country offers the only true picture of the national level of taste and interest. The plea was not, as Charles Angoff later asserted in his *Literary History of the American People*, to "do away with aesthetic criticism completely," but, rather, to give literature an understandable base in the life of society. All this is commonplace today, and even at the time a few students were groping in that direction; but to my knowledge the article was the first reasoned presentation of the case.

"The City in American History," in the *Mississippi Valley*

Historical Review, 1940, presented the thesis that the urban influence had played a vital role in the nation's development from earliest colonial times and had become the prime factor with the filling up of the country toward the end of the nineteenth century. This conception, though diminishing, did not seek to destroy the frontier theory but to substitute a balanced view: an appreciation of the significance of both country and city in the rise of American civilization. The need for such a revaluation had long been in my mind, perhaps as a result of having lived in towns, small, medium-sized, and large; and in a letter to me as early as 1925 Turner himself had foreseen the likelihood of "an urban reinterpretation." The piece, which Blake McKelvey in the *American Historical Review* twelve years later called "seminal," appeared at a timely moment, for in the intervening period McKelvey was able to report marked activity in the field. McKelvey, one of my Ph.D.'s, had himself by then published the first two of a four-volume history of Rochester, N.Y., where he holds the almost unique post of city historian.

"Biography of a Nation of Joiners," in the *American Historical Review*, 1944, traced by chronological stages the evolution of voluntary associations—those agencies of self-government outside the regular government—from the simple beginnings in colonial days to their all-pervasive place in modern times. It showed that the phenomenon was peculiarly American in its scope and political and social effects and underlay the traditional attachment to the doctrine of *laissez faire*. Historical writers had for many years recognized the importance of such organizations in specific situations but not their wider implications for American life as a whole. The article bore no apparent fruit, however, until Oscar Handlin, director of the Center for the Study of the History of Liberty in America at Harvard, announced a few years ago that the subject would be one of its major objects of inquiry. Incidentally, this is the only piece of mine to be cited in Supreme Court opinions (the Garner and Wieman cases in 1950 and 1952).

"A Dietary Interpretation of American History," in the *Proceedings* of the Massachusetts Historical Society, 1952, maintained that of the numerous explanations offered by scholars for men's actions—the religious urge, the economic motive, and the like—the most basic and unfortunately most neglected one was the human need for an adequate food supply. It demonstrated that in all periods, whether of peace or war, and including the very discovery of the New World, this quest had been an important when not the determining factor. Few historians, however, have chosen to follow up the lead.

"Tides of American Politics," in the *Yale Review*, 1939, set forth a cyclical theory of conservative and liberal tendencies in the national government and held that from the beginning of political parties onward the process has operated in obedience to an inherent rhythm, each trend averaging around sixteen years and being therefore presumably predictable. Understandably, the article excited much popular interest both then and since, with little questioning as to the validity of the analysis; nor to my knowledge has any historian disputed it. The St. Louis *Post-Dispatch*, however, objected, contending that so "mechanistic" an interpretation made us appear to be "ruled by the calendar" instead of "by our thinking," and thereby contravened "our concepts of democracy." According to a White House aide, David K. Niles—of whom more in the next chapter—President Franklin Roosevelt read the essay and the prospect it held out of the existing liberal era lasting till 1947 or 1948 helped him decide to run for a third term.

Less scholarly, even though involving a collaboration of scholars, was an article in *Life*, November 1, 1948. This reported the outcome of a poll I had taken of fifty-five historians,

rating the Presidents under five headings from "great" to "fail-
ure." A judgment of historians is not necessarily the judgment
of history, but at any given moment it is the best available
without awaiting the sifting process of time. Hence this piece
also evoked wide public interest. Scores of letters and postals,
not to mention newspaper editorials, registered anguish or as-
sent—mostly anguish. The main sticking point was the class-
ing of Franklin Roosevelt among the six "greats," next to
Lincoln and Washington and above Wilson, Jefferson, and
Jackson. Cried Edmund Proctor of New York City, for example, "I will agree that FDR was great if by that is meant
great liar, great faker, great traitor, great betrayer," while "A
100% American" (not otherwise identified) compared the rank-
ing to "what a Limburger cheese smells like." Besides blind
hatred of Roosevelt's policies, still so fresh in memory, the
virulence undoubtedly reflected also new Republican bitter-
ness over Truman's unexpected victory in the 1948 election,
which occurred almost simultaneously with the article's appearance.

Fourteen years later the poll was repeated in response to
persistent queries as to where the later incumbents, Truman
and Eisenhower, would stand, and I myself was curious as to
whether a longer perspective would confirm the earlier estimate of Roosevelt. The results of the 1962 inquiry, printed
in the New York *Times Magazine*, involved seventy-five
scholars and corroborated in general the previous judgments,
including that as to Roosevelt. The main difference was the
lowering of Andrew Jackson one notch from the least of the
"greats" to first of the "near greats." Truman also qualified as
near great, and Eisenhower came out next to the bottom—
eleventh—in the middle or average group. This time the out-
cries, though less numerous and violent, centered on the two
added ratings and again emanated from incredulous Republicans. If the historians were correct, however, every American
regardless of party could rejoice that great or near-great Presi-

dents have headed the Republic for nearly half its existence—
a tribute to government by the people and a record which any
nation might envy.

My initial book after going to Harvard was the second of
the two-volume college text which Homer C. Hockett and I
had tentatively planned at Ohio State and on which I had
been working at odd times since. It came out in June, 1925.
The dividing line was the year 1829, the advent of the age of
Jackson. As the title indicated, the *Political and Social History
of the United States* departed from the customary pattern
by giving the political story a social and cultural context. A
waggish friend observed, "The first volume is worthy of
Homer, the second a work of Art." The different approach
found a ready market, at once undercutting our chief compet-
itor, Bassett's *Short History of the United States*. Thanks to
the need to incorporate the multitudinous developments of
the advancing twentieth century, we revised the work in 1933
and again in 1941 and 1951, moving the original dividing line
by stages to 1865, the end of the Civil War; and each time,
of course, the concluding volume brought the account down
to the present. However, as rival texts fashioned on the same
model entered the field, adoptions gradually declined. But
even today, though the Korean intervention is the last topic to
be treated—an event of ancient history in this fast-moving age
—the set continues to sell.

Meanwhile, in 1944, at the publisher's initiative, Hockett
and I abridged the two volumes into one for use in single-
semester history courses; and this version, *Land of the Free*,
also did well for some years and is still in print. Then
the editors of *Information Please Almanac* asked me to tell
the over-all story in 5,000 words for their maiden issue in
1947. This was a sort of *reductio ad absurdum* and I was on
the point of refusing when it occurred to me that if I did not
do it somebody else certainly would and that it would be interesting to see what one could make of so preposterous an

assignment. As a matter of fact the first draft ran to but 3,500 words, leaving room to put a little flesh on the bones. Whatever else could be said of the result, it was at least a demonstration of concise exposition, and the yearbook continued to use it for a dozen years.

The *History of American Life*, a project originating, it will be remembered, in my last Iowa years, occupied the lion's share of my nonteaching time till the enterprise finally ground to completion. Dixon Ryan Fox and I as the editors had signed up the participants before I removed to Harvard —though two of them subsequently withdrew—and we now faced the task of seeing that they turned in manuscripts conforming to the series' pioneering conception. Besides Fox and myself, the eventual list consisted of Herbert I. Priestley, Thomas J. Wertenbaker, James Truslow Adams, Evarts B. Greene, John A. Krout, Carl Russell Fish, Arthur C. Cole, Allan Nevins, Ida M. Tarbell, Harold U. Faulkner, and Preston W. Slosson, all but Adams and Miss Tarbell in academic positions. In each case we scrutinized minutely the author's original draft for both substance and language and when necessary revised his final product. On me rested the additional responsibility of regularizing matters of technical form like citations and capitalization; and when Fox left Columbia to assume his exacting duties as president of Union College in 1934, I came to carry more and more of the burden of the scholarly and literary editing as well. Fox in fact would never have got his own book out except by securing Krout as his collaborator.

To our keen disappointment the volumes did not appear as rapidly as we had planned or even in chronological order. Four scattered ones were published in 1927 and the remaining eight trailed along at irregular intervals, the last in 1944. Most of the contributors were delayed by having to master and correlate unfamiliar material; the rest, contrary to their contractual obligations, let other writing take priority. Becker as editorial consultant constantly chided us for expending on other people's manuscripts energy which we might better be devoting to works of our own; and in similar vein Beard wrote me, "What a waste of your time. Break away as soon as you can." But Fox and I, despite spells of discouragement, were sustained by the faith that the undertaking would redirect the future course of American historical research and instruction. So slow, however, was the last of the twelve volumes in appearing that Macmillan asked for an additional one to carry the over-all account nearer to date. The thirteenth, Dixon Wecter's *The Age of the Great Depression,* came off the press in 1948. Incidentally, Wecter before tackling it had felt critical of Roosevelt's handling of the economic crash, but intensive study of the evidence resulted in his concluding that the New Deal measures were on balance a great humanitarian achievement.

My own volume—the eighth to be published—came out in January, 1933, having been held back by the time consumed on other manuscripts. *The Rise of the City, 1878-1898,* treated a period which historians had slighted except in its political phases; and it was only as my examination of the sources proceeded that I realized this span of years marked the emergence of urban centers as the dominant force in American civilization, "pulsating to the very finger-tips of the whole land," as a contemporary said. With that as the key the diverse social and cultural developments fell into an intelligible pattern. And since Miss Tarbell's parallel volume dealt with *The Nationalizing of Business* it was possible to do full justice to the thesis.

When ten volumes of the *History of American Life* had appeared, the American Historical Association paid it the unusual honor of devoting a general session to an appraisal of the enterprise at its 1936 convention in Providence, R.I. The participants, each a leader in his field, spoke from the angles of political history, literary history, and social history, with the final say falling to me. As evidenced in the published account, *Approaches to Social History* (1937), the verdict was forthright approval. All three in different words stressed the value of the series in "leavening the historical lump" and attributed the occasional faults of execution to the venture's pathbreaking nature. My own view of its significance was expressed in a memorandum requested by the Macmillan Company after the twelfth volume was out. It read in part:

Fox and I in planning this work aimed to free American history from its traditional servitude to party struggles, war and diplomacy and to show that it properly included all the varied interests of the people. . . . The editors believe they have accomplished their primary purpose and also a hardly less important secondary one. This was to stimulate scholarly research and teaching in the new aspects of history so indicated. A glance at the annual list of doctoral dissertation subjects in United States history shows the extent to which cultural themes have now come to occupy the attention of the rising generation. Courses in American social and intellectual history have also multiplied in the colleges and universities.

This assessment perhaps ascribed too much credit to the undertaking, since the closer association of history with the sister social sciences, to be noted later, had worked to the same end.

Aside from the *History of American Life* my editorial labors were only incidental. In 1928, with Morison as the moving spirit, a few of us founded the *New England Quarterly*, a "Historical Review of New England Life and Letters" designed for the interested lay public. This has involved through the years the reading of occasional manuscripts. For many years, too, I served on a committee of the Massachusetts Historical Society to oversee its *Proceedings* and other learned publications. In addition, the premature death in 1938 of a fellow historian and friend resulted in the editing of a work left in rough draft. Marcus Lee Hansen of the University of

Illinois, dying when but forty-five, had spent two decades gathering material, mostly in Old World archives, on the social and economic background of emigrant groups to America from colonial days to the Civil War; and in his last hours he expressed the wish that I put the manuscript into final shape or that it be destroyed—an alternative which would have entailed a grave loss to knowledge. *The Atlantic Migration, 1607-1860*, appeared in 1940, winning the Pulitzer Prize. In a desire to extend further the influence of a scholar cut off in his prime I also assembled in a small accompanying volume, *The Immigrant in American History*, nine of Hansen's interpretative essays, five of which had existed hitherto only in typescript.

In 1953 my edition of Frederick Law Olmsted's *The Cotton Kingdom* came out. This incomparable eyewitness report by a Northerner of human and economic conditions in the ante-bellum South had not been reprinted since 1862, though it was fundamental to an understanding of the sectional rift. Olmsted made three trips through the slave states in the 1850's, mingling with all classes white and black and jotting down day-by-day observations. My extensive introduction, based in part on his private correspondence and in part on his various published accounts, portrayed his unique fitness for the task and, for the first time, traced the tortuous evolution of the text of *The Cotton Kingdom*. Originating as on-the-spot articles for the New York *Times* and the New York *Tribune*, they had afterward been expanded into three bulky works and then, for more convenient reading, contracted into the final version. Helpful to historians in weighing his judgments was the documented demonstration that both before and after the Civil War he held moderate views of slavery and the race's innate capacity.

Of books of my own composing, the first after *The Rise of the City*—excluding two thorough revisions of the college text—was *Learning How to Behave, a Historical Study of*

American Etiquette Books. Published in 1946, it was the incidental result of idly picking up a hundred or so guides to polite conduct from colonial days on. Secondhand dealers in Cambridge and Boston, thinking the volumes had no more value than out-of-date almanacs, gladly disposed of them for a song. But as I examined the contents it became evident that the handbooks in the course of offering past evidences of social snobbery also mirrored the heightening position of women, the growing respect for children's rights, and, in general, the declining importance of class lines. In short, the story, apart from its quaint and trivial aspects, significantly revealed "the leveling-up process of democracy." Besides the works in my personal collection—which subsequently went to the Women's Archives at Radcliffe—the study rested on manuals in Boston and New York libraries and in the Library of Congress.

Three years later, in 1949, *Paths to the Present* followed. This was a set of thirteen essays which in the main were revisions of earlier printed ones plus some new ones on such varied themes as "The Martial Spirit" and "Persisting Problems of the Presidency." Among the revamped pieces were those on the city in American history, the significance of voluntary associations, the dietary influence, and the cycles of conservatism and liberalism in national affairs. For whatever reason, the volume, though to my mind a maturer performance than *New Viewpoints,* failed to arouse the same interest among the younger members of the profession. Could the less challenging title have been a factor? On the other hand, *Paths to the Present* was translated into French, Dutch, and Japanese, and the United States Information Agency circulated a shortened version in "easy to read" English in Greece, the Middle East, Burma, India, Japan, and West Africa.

The American as Reformer, published the next year, was a book I had never expected to write, although the subject had long intrigued me. It grew out of an invitation from President

E. Wilson Lyon of Pomona College at Claremont, Calif., to spend a week with the students and faculty and deliver three public addresses. I chose the topic because the portents of this later postwar era were pointing to a revival of the repressive forces which had assailed freedom of thought and action in the 1920's. The treatment took off from a passage of Madison's in No. 14 of *The Federalist*:

Is it not the glory of the people of America that, whilst they have paid a decent regard to the opinions of former times and other nations, they have not suffered a blind veneration for antiquity, for custom, or for names, to overrule the suggestions of their own good sense, the knowledge of their own situation, and the lessons of their own experience?

Then followed a consideration of the theme under three headings: "The Historical Climate of Reform," "The Reform Impulse in Action," and "The Revolt against Revolt." President Lyon's foreword to the printed lectures called them "a guide to sanity." Unfortunately they could not stay the gathering storm of McCarthyism and its attendant evils. For this more than the voice of a college professor was required.

The authoring of books constitutes the highest function of the historian, or so I believe. Otherwise his rigorous training and tireless probing of the past do not sufficiently repay society. Teaching communicates knowledge only to a limited circle, as do speeches, since the persons reached are relatively few, and in any event the spoken word quickly fades from memory. By the same token, articles, unless they are collected for easier reference between two covers, tend to get lost in the mounting files of periodicals. A book, on the other hand, addresses a potentially unbounded audience, not to mention generations unborn. And even if the work be narrow in scope it is readily available to specialists in the field. One of the failures of the history profession lies in the number of first-rate scholars who never get around to putting their findings into this more telling form. In my own case, writing has always been largely a matter of rewriting, a slow, painful, yet ever fascinating task. Hence it was comforting to learn that George Bancroft often penned ten drafts of a page, and even more so to hear Becker say that his relaxed and crystal style was the product of remorseless revision. Nonetheless I have never ceased to envy the fortunate souls from whom the right words flow smoothly.

Though I had done considerable book reviewing in pre-Harvard years, I now did less and less, finally stopping altogether. A conscientious performance not only consumed valuable time, but, as my friendship spread with colleagues over the country, it became increasingly hard to render objective judgments. My only major undertaking, indeed, was the co-operative *Dictionary of American Biography* for the *American Historical Review* as the twenty-one volumes issued from the press from 1928 to 1944. Except perhaps for the editors themselves probably nobody else has ever read the set through from beginning to end. Though I spotted occasional errors of fact, emphasis, and interpretation and was able to name eligible individuals who had been omitted, my over-all view was that the work represented a monumental achievement, its greatest usefulness for scholars lying in the sketches of minor characters of whom no full-length biographies existed. The long travail proved richly rewarding, for it enlarged my knowledge of the lesser figures who had helped build American civilization.

In a sense, membership on the advisory committee for the annual Pulitzer Prize in American history also constituted a sort of book reviewing. I served from 1937 to 1954 save for two years, one when my son's *Age of Jackson* was in the running, the other when abroad. Generally the committee judged approximately sixty books, recommending five in order of preference to the central body at Columbia, which, however, reserved the right to select one not on the list. During my incumbency they exercised this option only once, granting the award in 1945 to Stephen Bonsal's *Unfinished Business,* a firsthand record of the Paris Peace Conference, which in our judgment was the raw material of history rather than a sifted treatment. Otherwise our first choices usually prevailed. My chief criticism of the system was that entries which would have stood little chance against strong competitors could win out in a year when the going was easy.

As a matter of course I kept up my interest in professional organizations, indeed, helped bring two new ones into being. The Social Science Research Council, formed in 1924, climaxed a widespread feeling of the scholars in these branches that the growing specialization—"knowing more and more about less and less"—was erecting formidable barriers to a needed interchange of insights and skills. I was one of the two original members representing the American Historical Association and continued active until 1942, serving as chairman from 1930 to 1933. The moving spirits during this nearly score of years were Charles E. Merriam, Wesley C. Mitchell, Edmund E. Day, William F. Ogburn, Edwin F. Gay, Isaiah Bowman, Edwin B. Wilson, Robert Redfield, and Edwin G. Nourse, all leaders in their respective fields and men intellectually stimulating.

The Council's main projects involved co-operative research, a method unfruitful in historical investigation, where the best results have always been attained by "the lone man thinking." Nevertheless history, too, derived benefit from the program of fellowships and grants-in-aid for individual inquiries and from the holding of conferences of historians to canvass common problems. A series of these gatherings in 1931, for instance, considered the most promising leads for future historical study and the training of the qualified personnel. The one over which I presided listed twenty such themes in the American past. To give the deliberations of the various groups wider currency they were published in a book *Historical*

Scholarship in America: Needs and Opportunities (1932) and distributed generally through the profession.

An example seven years later, which perhaps reflected less credit on the participants, grew out of the Council's inviting each of its fields to make a thorough appraisal of some recent outstanding work in the interest of improving research methods. In the case of history the choice fell on *The Great Plains* by Walter P. Webb of the University of Texas. Preparatory to its evaluation by a conference under my chairmanship, Fred A. Shannon of the University of Illinois spent a summer on a dissection of the book. In checking Webb's sources he found pertinent ones Webb had overlooked and, more gravely, challenged the validity of his basic theses. When Webb was asked for his rebuttal he at first wrathily refused, branding the critique ignorant and malicious, then prepared one which he was persuaded to soften before it went with Shannon's analysis to the scholars who were to have the last say. In this still somewhat emotional rejoinder he stated among other things he had "never asserted that *The Great Plains* was history"; instead, it was "a work of art." The discussion at the conference proved animated but inconclusive, never coming to grips with Shannon's crucial points. Beneath the surface personal feelings ran strong, with some of the members obviously regarding the trenchant criticisms as breaching the canons of politeness. It made one wonder how well they maintained scholarly objectivity when viewing historical characters. A digest of the proceedings was published by the Council in its series *Critiques of Research in the Social Sciences* (1940). If Shannon's animadversions did any damage to Webb's professional standing or to his pride, the effects were only transient. In 1958 the American Historical Association elected him its president, and his official address staunchly avowed that the book "has never been revised" and "never will be revised by me."

The other scholarly agency I helped to establish stemmed from a feeling within the profession that the colonial era, forming the first half of American history, had been wrongly suffering from neglect. To the younger generation of historians it lacked appeal in view of the compelling attractions of the national period. Yet opportunities still abounded in many vital aspects of life and society which earlier writers had passed over. The chance to mend the situation arose in 1939 when Hunter D. Farish, one of my Ph.D.'s, became director of historical research for Colonial Williamsburg, the eighteenth-century Virginia capital which the Rockefeller millions were restoring. As a member of his advisory committee, with Charles M. Andrews, Sam Morison, and others, I assisted in assembling his research staff, providing grants-in-aid to interested outside scholars, and launching a publication program. From these beginnings there developed in 1945 the Institute of Early American History and Culture, supported jointly by Colonial Williamsburg and the College of William and Mary. Because Farish's health had meanwhile failed, Carl Bridenbaugh became the executive director; and I was the initial chairman. Under Bridenbaugh's vigorous leadership the Institute embarked on a range of activities far more extensive than had been possible under the original setup. I resigned, however, in March, 1947, confident that the organization was in excellent hands and that colonial history was rapidly regaining its rightful position as a field of inquiry.

The American Historical Association, of course, held my primary allegiance. I read papers before it and in the 1920's served on the Council. The Washington meeting of 1934 in particular stands out because of a talk one evening with William E. Dodd, then president. He had returned for the occasion from his post as ambassador to Germany. His account of dealings with Nazi officials came to mind some years later when in February, 1941, after his death, a day-by-day account of his Berlin experiences appeared in *Ambassador*

Dodd's Diary, edited by his son and daughter. Since he had expressly told me he was not finding leisure to keep a journal, the book took me by surprise, and I assumed, charitably, that the young people had pieced it together from the father's private letters to friends. When I suggested this in a letter to the son, who had sent me a copy, he made no reply. In any case passages in the book indicated that they could not have been set down at the time. The reviewers, however, took the work at face value.

In 1942 the Association elected me president. As America was then embroiled in World War II, the three-day convention scheduled for December at Columbus, Ohio, was to have centered about the theme "Civilization in Crisis"; but at the last minute the United States Office of Defense Transportation canceled the meeting, along with that of every other learned society, to clear the rails and airways for military uses. The alternative now was to hold none at all, as during World War I, or to hold a truncated one where a sizable local attendance would be certain. Fortunately the latter course proved feasible, for at the nation's capital a host of academic historians from all over the country were serving in government emergency agencies. The one-day affair consisted of a quick afternoon session for indispensable business and the official dinner in the evening at which the president spoke. My subject was "What Then Is the American, This New Man?," a query first posed by the French-born St. Jean de Crèvecœur in 1782. Published later in the *American Historical Review* and, slightly revised, in *Paths to the Present,* the address set forth a historical analysis of the national character, depicting it as having arisen out of the people's long-persisting pioneer and agrarian environment and then progressively modified by the advent of urbanism and industrialism. In honor of my election some eighty of my former Harvard and Iowa graduate students had commissioned the Boston artist Gardner Cox to paint my portrait, their spokesmen presenting it to me on my fifty-fourth birthday in Cambridge the preceding February. This is the continuing reminder of my moment of glory.

To add variety to the Harvard years there was a constant stream of interesting and worth-while visitors to Cambridge and the vicinity. They came to teach on temporary appointment or to deliver special lectures or to pursue research or for divers other reasons. Among them, Dexter Perkins of the University of Rochester, later of Cornell, spent summers with his wife on the old family estate in the town of Harvard within easy motoring distance of Widener Library. We had numerous interests in common both as to past and present developments in the United States. His mastery of American diplomatic history illumined many a dark corner for me, while his habit of weighing the pros and cons of current affairs often made him a more placid observer of them than I. Though our political outlook was much the same, he himself said he found it hard to stay indignant long.

Harold J. Laski of the London School of Economics showed up nearly every winter, stopping with Frankfurter until Felix went to the Supreme Court and then with one of his other old friends. To Harold, Harvard was a second home. He had taught there from 1916 to 1920, a mental quickener to both colleagues and students. In 1919, when he backed the Boston police in the strike which brought Governor Calvin Coolidge to factitious national prominence, President Lowell, though disapproving Laski's stand, had defended his right to take it and resisted strong pressure to dismiss him. All this, of course, antedated my own arrival. Smallish and slight with high forehead, tiny mustache, and coal-black hair, he possessed a gift of speech which served as half his battle in argument. As if deliberately avoiding his academic specialty of political theory, he discoursed engagingly as a man of the world, recounting his intimacy with celebrities in Europe and America. Though he sometimes unblushingly embroidered the facts, this foible we willingly condoned since it was evident he was merely seeking to make a good story better. Only rarely did he cast himself in the central role. An unforgettable instance during World War II was his graphic description of having been bombed when asleep in bed and blown from the fourth to the second floor of a hotel without any harm; but his wife after Harold's death in 1950 told his biographer that to her belief this had never actually occurred. As he probably knew from the newspapers—I myself having seen it in the New York *Times*—the experience had befallen someone else, so, he doubtless thought, why not him? His passing left his friends, who were legion in America, with a sense of keen personal loss.

Alfred A. Knopf, the New York publisher, proved a no less interesting visitor, though for wholly different reasons. Coming every year he entertained faculty members, predominantly historians, at Lucullan feasts in Boston marked by fine wines and choice cigars. Dark of skin, compactly built, and characteristically wearing a deep blue or red soft shirt with contrasting tie, Knopf tended to be laconic of speech but was always a catalyst to good conversation by his guests. Only under urging would he tell of his relations with authors, American and foreign, many of whom he had first brought to national attention. We admired Alfred particularly for publishing learned works which promised little or no financial return. He seemed indeed, as I said in a toast to him on one occasion, "Clio's boy friend." Politically he professed a gloomy outlook on mankind, but his dour words never quite concealed his underlying hope. The dinners appeared to have no ulterior purpose. In all the years I partook of his hospitality (and he gave similar parties annually at the American Historical Association) he never once asked for a manuscript. It was not till 1953 that I offered him one (Olmsted's *Cotton Kingdom*), which he accepted knowing full well it was a dubious money-making venture.

The most memorable evening with Alfred perhaps was one

Elizabeth shared when H. L. Mencken, then editor of the *American Mercury*, was the only other guest. From Mencken's acidulous writings we had expected to encounter an ogre, but, instead, the Baltimore iconoclast (who lost no opportunity to inform his readers that "all college professors are asses") turned out to be a charming companion, one who listened as well as talked. Although our paths never crossed again, letters did, as from time to time I sent him references from out-of-the-way historical sources for his monumental study of the American language. And after my presidential address on the evolution of the American national character, he wrote commending it, with a caveat, however, as to the future. "It seems to me," he said in typical vein,

that there has been a change in the constitution of the American population during the last generation and a half, and that it has been altogether for the bad. Here in Baltimore I live in a slum that is now crowded with war-working immigrants from the Appalachian chain. I thought I was familiar with these anthropoids, but I must now report that they are really much worse than I ever suspected. . . . The birth rate among them is enormous. In their native wilds there is some compensation in the high infant death rate, but here in Baltimore their young are being coopered and fostered at the public expense, so there'll be a vast supply of them hereafter. It is certainly not reassuring to look at them. . . . In all the world I have never seen a more degraded class of white men, not even in Southeastern Europe.

And he ended, as he usually did: "If you ever get into these wilds, I surely hope you let me hear of it. Life grows more and more uncomfortable, but nevertheless some really first rate saloons are still open."

In a special category was Associate Justice Louis D. Brandeis of the Supreme Court, whom I came to know, as in Laski's case, through Frankfurter. The Justice and his wife made it a practice to invite Elizabeth and me for dinner at the Hotel Bellevue in Boston while on their way to and from their summer place outside Chatham, and when we in turn went

to Cape Cod we always called on them. They lived unpreten-
tiously in a weather-beaten cottage on a scrubby knoll overlooking the ocean. In Brandeis's presence you sensed a noble
and gracious spirit. Far from parading his eminence, he
quietly drew you out, eliciting your very best by making you
feel your opinions counted. Tall and somewhat stooped,
with a strong, beautiful face and deep-set pensive eyes, he has
been likened to an Old Testament prophet, a true-enough
characterization except perhaps for an underlying quality of
gentleness.

The one subject I never felt free to broach was the Supreme
Court, but twice he himself penetrated the barrier. When
Franklin Roosevelt's nomination of Senator Hugo Black to the
tribunal in 1937 evoked nationwide criticism, in which President Lowell joined, Brandeis quietly remarked that from long
personal acquaintance he considered the Alabamian thoroughly well qualified. His prescience came strikingly to mind
when Black's eight colleagues in 1962, in an unusual ceremony
commemorating his quarter-century of service, listened ap-
provingly to the United States Solicitor General acclaim the
"extraordinarily great contributions" he had made "to the
country, to the law and to the Court." Again, when Roosevelt
sought to overcome the hostility of the majority of the Justices
to New Deal measures by adding younger men to offset those
aged seventy or older, the octogenarian Brandeis, in no sense
himself one of the offenders, expressed the view that the conservative mentality is a product of genes rather than of years,
that in fact age, with its accompaniment of financial security,
tends to emancipate judges from the economic pressures and
illiberal predilections which may have conditioned their
previous thinking. Though Congress rejected the plan, the
Court, it will be remembered, in some alarm hastily reversed
its course. As Reed Powell pointed the moral, "A switch in time
saves nine."

The Justice talked freely of books he was reading, displayed lively interest in Harvard, and fondly recalled his Boston career, dwelling with particular satisfaction on his fight to establish state savings-bank life insurance. Reminiscence after reminiscence unconsciously footnoted his credo: "The irresistible is often only that which is not resisted." I knew him, of course, in his contemplative years, when he was no longer "the people's counsel" working without fee for the public good. The trait called greatness is an elusive one, but if it comprehends humility, moral majesty, faith in the common folk, deep human compassion, and constancy of purpose—in short, the quality of having made the world better for having lived in it—then Brandeis alone of the men I have known fulfilled the requirements.

VIII

Calls of Citizenship

Living on the Eastern seaboard brought me more directly in touch with public issues and events than the relative isolation of Iowa had made possible. My earliest contact came about through the Ford Hall Forum, an institution of civic-minded Bostonians which provided a platform for speakers of all shades of political and social opinion. In a city notorious for book banning and like forms of censorship it defiantly upheld the motto: "Let There Be Light." The connection arose by chance, resulting from a talk I had given to a summer gathering at Siasconset on Nantucket Island in September, 1924, on the eve of going to Harvard. In it I had set forth, for the first time publicly, the cyclical operation of American politics— delineated more fully years later in the *Yale Review* article— and the forecast of the probable duration of the current Coolidge-style conservatism till around 1932 elicited from a member of the group an anguished cry of "My God!" Afterward he introduced himself as David K. Niles, executive director of the Forum. A man about my own age, soft-spoken and of average build, it was through him that I became a member. Needless to say, neither of us that night dreamed that Dave himself would be part of the predicted resurgence of liberalism, moving to Washington first to help Harry Hopkins with President Roosevelt's emergency relief program, then serving as White House adviser on minority problems.

The Forum meetings, held on Sunday evenings, consisted of an hour-long address followed by an hour of lively discussion; the audiences were composed mainly of middle-aged folk of immigrant background. I presided on occasion and now and then delivered the talk. Once, when sudden illness obliged Morris Hillquit to cancel his engagement and I replaced him at the last moment, Reuben L. Lurie relates in his history of the Forum that a woman entering late glanced worriedly at the platform and ejaculated, "Morris, how you have changed!" Another time, after Mayor Curley had forbidden Margaret Sanger to hold forth on birth control in the city, we gave a banquet in her honor. When her turn came to speak, I as toastmaster ceremoniously placed a gag on her mouth and then, from a paper she passed me, read the remarks in her stead. Among those present to protest Curley's denial of free speech were Clarence Darrow and Morris Ernst, the widely known libertarian lawyers, and William Lloyd Garrison's grandson, Oswald Garrison Villard of the New York *Nation*. My association with the Forum, which continued unbroken until Niles departed for Washington, acquainted me with a type of Bostonian, mentally alert and largely self-educated, whom I otherwise would never have met.

Massachusetts also brought my first real knowledge of the Sacco-Vanzetti affair. In April, 1920, four and a half years before my arrival, the two obscure Italian workmen had been arrested, and the next year tried and sentenced to death, for robbing and killing a shoe-factory paymaster and his guard at South Braintree, near Boston. The postwar Red Scare was then at its peak, and the two men bore the stigma, prejudicial even in normal times, of being unnaturalized foreigners, wartime slackers, anarchists, and atheists. The foreman of the jury, according to later sworn testimony, had declared in advance of the trial that regardless of the evidence "They ought to hang them anyway"; and the presiding judge, Webster Thayer, while appeals from the sentence were still pending, had called them "anarchistic bastards" to a Dartmouth professor. In Iowa the cursory press notices of the case had made slight impression on me, but in Harvard circles the interest was keen, for Felix Frankfurter and many other trusted colleagues believed that the men were innocent or, in any event, had failed of a fair trial. In their considered opinion, which I quickly came to share, hysteria and bias had negated the precious American heritage of due process of law. To add to the sense of outrage, repeated motions for a new trial upon the uncovering of additional evidence were uniformly rejected by Judge Thayer, who under the Massachusetts law of the time had the say in the matter. A flagrant instance occurred in November, 1925, when a member of the notorious Morelli gang in Providence, R.I., awaiting the death sentence for a different murder, confessed that he and others of the band had committed the South Braintree crimes.

Excitement over the fate of Sacco and Vanzetti mounted not only locally, but through the nation and presently around the globe. As I was to say some twenty years after in the foreword to a book on the case—of which more later—the affair

created an atmosphere of popular tension, dread and crisis without parallel in Massachusetts annals since the exiling of Roger Williams and Anne Hutchinson and the witch persecutions of the seventeenth century. To duplicate its national repercussions one would have to go back to the trial of the Chicago anarchists for the Haymarket bombing in the 1880's, and for its world effects to the Dreyfus case in France near the turn of the century.

Adding to the ferment, Frankfurter in February, 1927, published a little volume *The Case of Sacco and Vanzetti, a Critical Analysis for Lawyers and Laymen*, which exposed point by point the weakness and the misuse of the evidence against them.

Several weeks later a student of mine, Gardner ("Pat") Jackson, who had resigned from the Boston *Globe* to take advanced work at Harvard, consulted me as to the advisability of dropping his studies in order to devote all his time to the Sacco-Vanzetti Defense Committee. I heartily approved with the words, as Pat recalls them: "I only *teach* social history, but you will be helping to *make* it." Through him I came to know Aldino Felicani, an Italian-born job printer in Boston, tall, broad-shouldered, and stolid-faced, who had organized the Defense Committee and, like Sacco and Vanzetti, was himself a philosophical anarchist. Pat's particular function was to rally public opinion by spreading far and wide Frankfurter's criticisms, which he did with great imagination and skill. From time to time he sought my advice as to tactics and particularly as to leaders in the academic world who might be enlisted in the cause. Governor Alvan T. Fuller's last-minute appointment of an advisory committee of three to review the evidence, headed by Harvard's President Lowell, was in part the fruit of this agitation and seemed for the moment to promise that the lives of the men might yet be spared. But the committee, while rebuking Judge Thayer for injudicious conduct, unanimously upheld the jury's verdict.

Lowell's role in this proceeding—for he was the dominating figure—is one of the more puzzling aspects of the whole episode. Subsequent analyses of the committee's report by legal scholars revealed faulty reasoning and the suppression of vital testimony favorable to the men. Like many a lesser human being, Lowell doubtless could not surmount the unconscious prejudices due to his station in life, a high and secure one by New England standards. He had indeed given evidence of this earlier. As a hereditary Republican he had in 1920 signed the appeal of thirty-one party notables for the election of Harding on the improbable ground that this would best assure America's entrance into the League of Nations. As a Boston Brahmin he had, shortly before my going to Harvard, vainly sought to induce the faculty to restrict the admission of Jewish students. And, it will be remembered, he had asked the History Department to recall the invitation to a temporary post extended to Salvemini, the foe of Fascism. One can only suppose that a Massachusetts patrician of inherited wealth could not, even while striving to do so, weigh dispassionately the innocence or guilt of "a good shoemaker and a poor fish peddler," both of lowly foreign birth. As Frankfurter notes in his published reminiscences, John F. Moors, a classmate and long-time friend of Lowell's, considered him "incapable of seeing that two wops could be right and the Yankee judiciary could be wrong." Yet in the purely intellectual realm, where his emotions were not engaged, he was almost invariably fair-minded, sagacious, and farsighted. It was these qualities that made him one of Harvard's great presidents.

The publication of the Lowell report lowered a curtain on any further discussion of the merits of the case in the Boston press. For example, I wrote a letter to the newspapers (August 11, 1927), which read in part:

There is no justice or fair play in a court system which can deny to men condemned to death on circumstantial evidence the opportunity of a judicial review of the facts of the case. . . . It is for this reason that the conscience of countless high-minded men and women remains disquieted by the outcome of the Governor's inquiry. When the passions of the hour have subsided and this phase of the situation emerges into sharper relief, the great body of informed opinion of the commonwealth will unquestionably insist on changing the present system so as to safeguard this fundamental human right. Meantime . . . Sacco and Vanzetti will have died as the victims of an anachronistic legal system.

And that in fact is just what the legislature quietly did in 1939. But my letter, like doubtless innumerable others, never saw the light of print.

As August 22, the day of the electrocution, approached, men

and women gathered from far and near for a last frantic demonstration of protest. Jackson and Felicani, averse to emotional outbursts and relying to the end on the force of reason, did their best to sit on the lid and to a degree succeeded. I had some notion of their problems when John Dos Passos stormed into my Widener study and, after hastily introducing himself, solemnly proposed that he dress up like Paul Revere and ride through the countryside shouting "Save Sacco and Vanzetti!" Only with difficulty was he persuaded that the tactics of 1775 did not suit the year 1927.

Out of these agonizing days arose a lasting friendship with Pat Jackson, who after his part of the agitation could find no newspaper job in Boston and within a few years moved to Washington. There he has played an active role in practically every movement for economic and social reform from the New Deal era on. Of medium height, bespectacled, and gregarious, this son of a Colorado banker offers a striking contrast in attitude to that of Lowell, for, though Pat also inherited substantial means, his every instinct has been to help the poor and forlorn. Some might call it a sense of *noblesse oblige,* a term, however, which he himself would decry. Possibly the seed was planted by the fact his mother was a niece of Helen Hunt Jackson, the great nineteenth-century champion of the American Indian, who had been his father's first wife. Years after Pat left Boston, when I too became concerned about the plight of the red man, I found that this was also one of his countless interests. In Washington he made friends with important public figures; and when Elizabeth and I have visited him and his attractive helpmate Dorothy, we have met many of them at their table. To him they are, above everything else, the means of rectifying abuses shameful in a democratic society. The veteran newspaperman Homer Dodge once told him with affection, "Pat, the underdog has you on a leash."

For five years following the deaths of Sacco and Vanzetti a Memorial Committee, of which I was a member with Pat,

Felicani, and others, sought to keep alive public concern over their fate by staging at the Old South Church annual observances of August 22 with speakers of national note. Then the deepening of the Great Depression suspended the meetings until 1937, the tenth anniversary. The approach of war and its advent next intervening, we made the twentieth anniversary, in 1947, the occasion of tendering to Governor Robert Bradford for erection on Boston Common a giant bas-relief of the men by Gutzon Borglum. An honorary committee, including Albert Einstein, Mrs. Franklin D. Roosevelt, and Dean Wesley A. Sturges of the Yale Law School, sponsored the project, and a local committee of which I was chairman made the offer in person. The governor, seated in his office not far from the site of the statue which a repentant commonwealth had reared to Anne Hutchinson, said with apparent regret that in view of the almost certain public reaction the time had not yet come when an elected official could prudently take the step.

The next year G. Louis Joughin and Edmund M. Morgan published their important book *The Legacy of Sacco and Vanzetti*, for which I wrote the introduction. Morgan, a Harvard Law School professor and a nationally recognized authority on the law of evidence, dispassionately dissected the voluminous court testimony and concluded that the men had been "the victims of a tragic miscarriage of justice." Joughin, professor of literature at the New School for Social Research, for his part, reviewed the abundant literature evoked by the case —legal treatises, poems, plays, novels, and the like—which had rendered a similar verdict.

But by that time so many horrors had afflicted the world— mass exterminations, slave-labor camps, the ruthless displacement of whole populations—that it seemed as though the lot of two insignificant individuals in Massachusetts back in the 1920's could no longer prick the public conscience. This, however, did not prove to be the fact, probably because, whatever the malpractices of totalitarian regimes, Americans could not escape a sense of responsibility for what they themselves had permitted to happen. At any rate, in 1959 Alexander J. Cella, a member of the Massachusetts legislature born two years after the executions, introduced a resolution asking Governor Foster Furcolo to grant a posthumous pardon to Sacco and Vanzetti. The hearing, conducted by a joint committee of the two chambers—the first ever held on the merits of the trial —lasted from ten in the morning till nearly midnight, with all but one of the thirteen witnesses supporting the recommendation. In my own testimony I noted that Frankfurter, suspected of radicalism when he had written his book on the case, had as a Justice of the Supreme Court reaffirmed his stand by letting the volume be reprinted in 1954, twenty-seven years later. The audience in the crowded hall, largely persons too young to have had an emotional stake in the affair, seemed puzzled that there should be any doubt as to the course now to be followed. The committee in its report asserted, "We neither condone nor criticize the action taken by the courts," then sidestepped the question at issue on the specious ground that the power to grant clemency was an executive, not a legislative, function. The resolution, of course, was no more than a request to the governor. It seems likely that sooner or later the lawmakers will take the desired action, in which case it is improbable that the governor of that day will fail to comply.

The first presidential contest in which I took some part in Massachusetts was that of 1928 between Herbert Hoover and Alfred E. Smith; in 1924 when supposedly a temporary resident I had voted by mail in Iowa. If I had not already believed Hoover to have shown himself unduly friendly to business as Secretary of Commerce, Frankfurter's admiration of Smith's liberal record as four-time governor of New York might well have swung me to the Democrat—a feeling Felix documented by presenting me with a volume of Smith's speeches. The objections to Al's Catholicism also proved offensive as violating the constitutional principle of the separation of church and

state, nor did his being a "wet" bother me in view of the evil
fruits of prohibition in practice. Forty of us on the Harvard
faculty enthusiastically signed a public statement for him. Yet
one night when the former East Side boy, speaking over what
he called "the raddio," twice said "the secession of immigration" instead of "the cessation of immigration," it sorely tried
Elizabeth's allegiance. A few weeks later, however, when he
addressed a meeting in Boston she joined in lustily singing
"East Side, West Side," Smith's rallying song. I also helped
Dave Niles and others of the Ford Hall Forum organize the
Massachusetts Independent Voters Association, which supported Al with speakers, campaign buttons and stickers and
secured him such publicity as was possible in Boston's Repub-
lican-oriented press.

Smith's overwhelming defeat in the nation—the result of
prosperity, prejudice, and prohibition—did not prevent Massachusetts from going Democratic for President for the first
time since 1912. Several months afterward, at Frankfurter's
initiative, Al came to Boston as the dinner guest of the academics who had declared for him. The group additionally included our colleague the English philosopher Alfred North
Whitehead, who, though precluded from casting a ballot for
the New Yorker, shared our opinion of him. Smith in his talk
ignored the recent unpleasantness to discuss with wisdom and
authority the opportunities for public service which lay, often
unheeded, in the state realm. To our delight he disregarded
what might have seemed to a lesser man our formidable book
learning. The occasion fully confirmed our judgment of his
unusual natural powers.

By the time of the 1932 campaign the country was mired in
the Great Depression. The vaunted Hoover doctrine of rugged
individualism had yielded innumerable ragged individuals.
Months before the Democrats nominated Franklin D. Roosevelt to oppose Hoover's re-election, Frankfurter began reciting
his merits and warning against Walter Lippmann's demeaning

remarks in his syndicated column. In any case the economically prostrate land, it seemed to me, clearly required a change of parties and a more resilient chief executive, precisely what the Democratic standard-bearer offered in his promised "New Deal." As in 1928, a group of us at Harvard announced for the Democrat, and I assisted in reactivating the Massachusetts Independent Voters Association in his behalf. On election day Roosevelt carried both Massachusetts and the nation. For the first time since Woodrow Wilson a liberal political administration had come to power.

To avoid tedious repetition, suffice it to say that these twofold tactics—group faculty endorsements and the revivifying of the MIVA—furthered the cause in each of FDR's three successful later campaigns. In 1936 no fewer than eighty-one Harvard professors declared for him. Although others of our colleagues undoubtedly felt strongly to the contrary, for some reason they never chose to take a public stand. In 1944, his last race, I also joined, on Sidney Hillman's invitation, the pro-Roosevelt National Citizens Political Action Committee.

Of Roosevelt's four Republican opponents Wendell Willkie in 1940 made the greatest appeal to me. I liked his forthrightness, his courageous support of the administration's policy toward the Axis powers, and also what he avowed to be his basic acceptance of its reform measures. But I did not think he would be able to master the reactionary elements in his party, and I bridled at his and their uproar over a third term for the President. It appeared no time to switch captains with the nation teetering on the brink of global war. Yet Willkie warned his audiences that, if they ignored the custom, "our democratic system will not outlast another four years." I believed then, as I continue to do, that the electorate should have the option to keep a chief magistrate in office as long as it approves of him —a matter discussed at some length in a chapter of *Paths to the Present.* Hence the Twenty-second Amendment, adopted in 1951 in retrospective vengeance against Roosevelt, has seemed to me a denial of democracy, a decision which the country may someday in a time of crisis have cause to regret.

I met Willkie for the first time a year and a half after his defeat when we both received honorary degrees at Union College. A large, tousled-haired man bursting with vitality, he had been a Republican only since 1932; and his conversation revealed that at heart he was still the liberal-minded Democrat who, as he proudly mentioned, had stumped the country after World War I on behalf of the League of Nations. The only other time was shortly after Dewey in 1944 killed his chances of a Republican renomination in the Wisconsin primaries. Dining with several of us in Boston, he expressed deep distrust of his successful rival on the ground of his lack of rooted principle. Though Roosevelt, Willkie said, had done many things he did not like, Roosevelt did have a true sense of direction. In fact, he all but stated he would declare for him in the fall at the most telling point of the campaign. Whether he actually would have remains uncertain, for he died a month before election day.

Throughout the epochal Roosevelt era Frankfurter, though remaining in Cambridge until going to the Supreme Court, enjoyed close relations with the White House. He became a sort of minister without portfolio, giving advice and helping to draft legislation and to staff New Deal agencies—activities of which he said little to his Harvard colleagues. I myself met Roosevelt only once, and that time hardly counts, for it was in 1928 when he accompanied Al Smith on his campaign trip to Boston; but in our brief chat his warm personality made an abiding impression. As chief executive his threefold program of relief, recovery, and reform had my undeviating approval. Even when liberal friends charged him with moving too slowly or with needlessly yielding ground, I trusted his superb sense of timing and a virtuosity of leadership which knew how to obtain the best results feasible.

Most of all, he impressed me in his role of public instructor, possessing an unmatched gift of simplifying and humanizing great and complicated questions for the common understanding. His "fireside chats" over the radio took his hearers, so to speak, into partnership, explaining his hopes and plans and imbuing them with his own confidence that with their support the problems would be solved. No previous President, not even Wilson, the erstwhile college professor, had shown so enlightened a conception of the office. At one stage, in 1935, when he seemed to be slighting this function, I wrote him of my disappointment, entrusting the letter to Frankfurter to ensure its reaching his eyes. Within less than a week he replied,

I agree with you about the value of regular reporting. My difficulty is a strange and weird sense known as "public psychology." No one has yet diagnosed it or even succeeded in listing its general principles. . . . I think from now on you will have to listen to me a little more frequently. . . .

My son Arthur comments on this exchange in *The Politics of Upheaval*, the third volume of his *Age of Roosevelt*.

As the New Deal forged ahead, dangers to the peace won at such tremendous cost in World War I thickened round the globe. In Europe Hitler's Germany and Mussolini's Italy embarked on their aggressions, while in Asia Japan emulated their course. As early as October, 1937, Roosevelt warned in his "quarantine" speech at Chicago that the "state of international anarchy" imperiled America's own security; but the public at large, still unsure of food and jobs, shrugged off overseas menaces. Like many others across the land, however, I helped bring victims of Nazi persecution to the United States by standing sponsor for them to the State Department; and their stories, added to the ominous newspaper accounts of conditions, filled me with mounting dread. Then on September 3, 1939, Britain and France declared war on Germany, the most blatant offender. The second world struggle in a single generation thus began, with Italy entering as Germany's partner some months later.

In the United States, opinion divided sharply over whether to regard the conflict as a matter of no concern or, on the contrary, to stretch our neutrality to the limit of extending all possible assistance to the ill-prepared Western Allies. In short, one's stand depended on whether he believed the triumph of totalitarianism abroad would jeopardize America's own ideals and institutions. As for my own attitude, I wrote on September 28 to a friend on the staff of the New York *Times,*

I want to do everything to help the Allies (however gross their sins) short of going to war, and I think I am willing to go to war if and when the so-called democracies should be on the point of being knocked completely out. As the father of two sons, I should want to be thoroughly convinced, however, that the critical juncture had actually arrived.

No isolationist sentiment was evident in Harvard circles, but the opposite was true of Boston. Out of morbid curiosity Elizabeth and I attended one of the "America First" meetings. The crowd, predominantly of Irish extraction, obviously cared nothing for Germany but raged and roared at the thought of helping England.

In June, 1940, when the Nazis overran France and only a badly crippled Britain remained to resist, more than a hundred members of the faculty and their wives joined together to form an organization called American Defense, Harvard Group. Ralph Barton Perry was the chairman and I served on the steering committee. We urged immediate entry into the struggle, feeling deeply that the fate of the United States as well as that of the Allies was now at stake. Weekly meetings devised means of spreading this conviction through speakers, newspapers, magazines, and the radio, and we kept up a stream of letters to important Washington figures. Our historians and political scientists provided most of the ammunition, and the Nieman Fellows co-operated by seeing that the language used was not too professorial.

Like countless other Americans, Elizabeth and I were listening on Sunday afternoon, December 7, 1941, to the weekly broadcast of the New York Philharmonic Symphony Orchestra when a voice broke in with the news of the Japanese daybreak attack on Pearl Harbor and the almost total destruction of our fleet. The dreaded crisis had come at last from an unexpected quarter. The next morning as I walked to my first course I wondered what I could say to the boys, whether indeed a man of fifty-three, himself exempt from military duty, could properly say anything. At least one of the group, Kenneth Stewart, a Nieman Fellow—and hopefully others— found my fumbling words appropriate. In a book published a few years later he wrote,

I went as usual to Arthur Schlesinger's class in the Social and Intellectual History of the United States. . . . He told them how wars had come before and how we had met them, how Harvard and our educational institutions had served to win the wars and had survived, how the cultural values which the students were there absorbing were the very things that we were fighting about and how we must conserve them while we fought. Some of you, he said, will go into the service at once, and you should. The war must be won first on the battlefronts. Others will be needed more than ever to develop the technical and scientific skills without which a war like this cannot be carried on. The rest of us will bide our time, keep education alive, do our immediate jobs as best we can, be ready to serve where we are needed most when the call comes. Then he picked up the thread of American history where he had dropped it at the end of the last hour.

Within three days Germany and Italy lined up with Japan, and America faced powerful foes on two sides of the globe.

Each year of the conflict reduced the number of civilian students. One semester my seminar, normally oversubscribed, had but two registrants—a Harvard 4-F and a Radcliffe girl— both of whom, despite the atmosphere of tension, produced papers of such excellence as later to be published. By contrast, students in army or navy uniform multiplied, though they remained only long enough to prepare for specialized duties.

The war, needless to say, also reached into the Schlesinger home. Tom, a third-year man at Brown University, enlisted in July, 1942, without waiting to be drafted, and from August, 1944, onward fought as an infantry private in France and Germany. He returned in July, 1945, after Germany's surrender, with three battle stars but physically unscathed; and he spent that month with us in Cambridge on furlough while his division, stationed in Mississippi, waited to be sent to Japan. The War Department, however, intervened at the last minute to substitute troops who had not yet seen action.

Arthur, who in June, 1942, was completing his three years in Harvard's Society of Fellows, joined the Office of War Information in Washington, later transferring to the Office of Strategic Services. The OSS, desiring early in 1944 to send him abroad, sought a navy commission for him, but the Naval Bureau of Personnel refused, alleging that he failed to meet the "overall requirements." This vague phrase covered the fact, as he learned from other sources, that he was deemed untrustworthy for having favored intervention in the war at too early a stage (for example, while connected with the Harvard Defense Group) and, further, because of the suspicion that his father was a Communist. This latter notion derived from the fact that I had signed a petition to Roosevelt back in 1937 to lift the arms embargo against the Spanish republicans who, with some Communist aid, were waging a losing fight with General Franco's Fascist-backed forces. All this seems bizarre in retrospect, but it reflected the well-meant if misguided efforts of persons who believed they were acting in a spirit of the highest patriotism. Arthur eventually served overseas for the OSS in an army private's uniform, being variously stationed in London and Paris and then, after the German collapse, in Wiesbaden. Fortunately he, too, escaped unharmed, though he was in London at the time the Nazi V-1 and V-2 bombs were pounding the city.

On the home front Elizabeth and I tried to contribute our

mite. Elizabeth assisted in the sale of war bonds, helped outfit rest rooms in nearby camps, and acted as a hostess in the only Boston recreation center open to soldiers and sailors regardless of race. We also had servicemen for Sunday dinner and regularly attended meetings of the Harvard Defense Group, now engaged in marshaling support for the administration's war measures. I further donated blood periodically to the Red Cross, and wrote articles for the *New Republic,* drawing on great moments in America's past to illuminate the present situation.

Feeling also a duty to future scholars and remembering the Ohio Historical Commission's accomplishments on a local scale some twenty years earlier, I wrote Frankfurter in Washington even before America's entry deploring "the inadequacy of the records of past wars, particularly in regard to nonmilitary governmental activities," and urging that, in view of what almost certainly impended, advance provision be made for attaching a historian to every wartime agency not only to see that routine records were faithfully kept but also to

make his own memoranda at staff meetings; encourage officials to discuss their problems with him; try to keep a personal journal of their daily doings; and, in general, seek to capture data which might throw light on the behind-the-scenes workings of the organization.

Besides ensuring a truer picture for posterity, the information might yield value to the government itself in the unfortunate event of later similar struggles. Felix, though greeting the proposal "with enthusiasm," felt he was not the one to act in the matter. "Despite those veracious sources of history—the columnists—I do not run this government," he wrote.

Others, however, both in and out of the administration seized on the idea and in March, 1942, the Bureau of the Budget, at the President's direction, set up an Advisory Committee on Records of War Administration with me as a member. Meetings occurred every few months, and to attend from

Cambridge sometimes proved difficult because of the reduction in the number of passenger trains and for a period the removal of all sleeping cars. Our major problems concerned the recruitment of qualified persons and the reluctance of some agencies to assume extra duties. Probably no historical officer performed all the functions desired, but by the end of 1944 forty-one agencies had instituted special units which were chronicling the emergency activities with a fullness never before known. Ten months after Japan's surrender the Committee, declaring that "the purpose for which it was established has been largely realized," went out of existence.

Meanwhile, in September, 1943, a fortuitous circumstance brought about a meeting with Winston Churchill. The great British Prime Minister, after a conference with Roosevelt in Washington, had come to Cambridge to receive an honorary degree, and as a break in the day's round of formalities he asked President Conant to arrange a half hour or so with some Harvard historians. Puffing a huge cigar and seeming utterly relaxed, he could not have been more affable; but it soon developed that his mind was less on times gone by than on the history he himself was helping to make, and in us of course he possessed avid listeners. The war, he observed, was proving exceedingly long and stubborn because Germany fought from interior lines, whereas the Allies had had to dissipate their strength by closing in from outside. With the tide now beginning to turn in our favor, however, he thought the Germans would show poor staying qualities. If the Nazi leaders to save their skins then fled to neutral Switzerland, the Allies, he said, would not go in after them but would suspend all trade until the Swiss expelled them. He added, with a sort of smile, that he personally would not be satisfied unless Hitler met death in the electric chair, since the truly great figures of history had lost their lives by hanging or the guillotine and only gangsters and criminals by electrocution. He talked with such evident unrestraint that he appeared to admit us to his innermost confidence. We of course should have known better. The newspapers later that week brought the word that Italy had secretly surrendered three days before the session, a fact he had omitted to mention.

An event of the next year I look back upon with self-reproach. This was the expulsion of the Frenchman Bernard Faÿ as a corresponding member of the Massachusetts Historical Society. Faÿ had taught in the Romance Languages Department at Iowa one summer, and I had encountered him again from time to time in Cambridge on his many lecture tours of the United States. Lamed in World War I, he was a broadly cultivated man and an engaging conversationalist. His life of Benjamin Franklin, published in 1929, though an American best-seller, had struck me as shallow and ill-informed, and unfortunately he asked for my opinion. Upon my replying that some of his crucial interpretations lacked adequate supporting evidence, he had heatedly retorted, "Be assured, Schlesinger, that the historians of the next fifty years will prove beyond doubt everything I have said." This novel doctrine of future verification naturally left me unmoved. With the fall of France the Nazi-controlled Vichy government made Faÿ director of the Bibliothèque Nationale in recognition of his pro-German leanings. It was this collaboration with the enemy which actuated the Historical Society, with only my colleague in the Law School, Zechariah Chafee, Jr., as I remember, dissenting, on the ground that, whatever Faÿ's political sins, the scholarly qualifications which had caused his election remained unaltered. Always stalwart in defense of freedom of opinion, he contended that the dismissal reflected wartime hysteria. I have never ceased to regret not siding with him, and I probably would have but for my low estimate of Faÿ as a historian, which, of course, was not the question at issue.

The last year and a half of the fighting saw me engaged in an enterprise which dealt with conditions essential to the nation's well-being in both peace and war. This was the Commission on Freedom of the Press, instituted and largely financed by *Time-Life-Fortune*. The members, besides myself, were Chafee, William E. Hocking, the Harvard philosopher, Archibald MacLeish, the Librarian of Congress, John M. Clark, the Columbia economist, Harold D. Lasswell and John Dickinson, respectively of the Yale and Pennsylvania Law Schools, Reinhold Niebuhr of the Union Theological Seminary, President George N. Shuster of Hunter College, Beardsley Ruml of the Federal Reserve Bank in New York, with the others from the University of Chicago: Robert Redfield in anthropology, Charles E. Merriam in political science, and President Robert M. Hutchins as chairman. Purposely, no member was himself connected with the press, the whole point being to judge its performance from the standpoint of the public for which it existed. I had never before been intimately associated with so diversely gifted and intellectually challenging a group. And, despite Hutchins's reputation for arbitrariness in dealing with his university faculty, he presided over the Commission with the utmost fairness and consideration.

Beginning in February, 1944, we assembled about every two months for several days at a time, usually in Chicago; and between sessions a research staff gathered relevant data. From the start the Commission construed the word "Freedom" in its title to mean immunity from every sort of undue pressure and extended the word "Press" beyond newspapers to include the radio, motion pictures, magazines, and books. (Television, that giant of the future, was then still struggling for birth.) Over the three years of our existence we heard the testimony of 58 individuals from the various mass media, and the staff recorded interviews with some 225 others. The basic question, as we saw it, was how to make the agencies of communication serve better the public interest without the government imposing restraints which in a democratic society might in the long run work more harm than good.

Our conclusions were summarized in *A Free and Responsible Press,* published in March, 1947. Underscoring the need for freeing the press "from the influences which now prevent it from supplying the communication of news and ideas needed," the Commission stated there were "no simple solutions." We, however, outlined thirteen ways in which the government, the public, and the press itself could, and should, in their various capacities assist the process, stressing that the cure rested primarily "on the elements of society acting directly on the press and not through governmental channels." One means suggested was a revival of the vigorous crossfire of criticism which had once characterized newspapers, but perhaps the single most important proposal was for the creation of an independent agency, privately financed, to appraise and report annually on the performance of the several media. A group of monographic studies on special aspects of the problem accompanied the report.

The predominant editorial reaction ranged from derision to denunciation. Not even the magazines which had underwritten the inquiry expressed approval, *Time,* for example, declaring that "the time and money and the caliber of the men" should have produced something less "disappointing." The Chicago *Tribune* headlined its article A FREE PRESS (HITLER STYLE) SOUGHT FOR U.S. TOTALITARIANS TELL HOW IT CAN BE DONE, which prompted the Chicago *Sun* to rejoin, "The *Tribune*'s account is itself a pretty conclusive documentation of the Commission's charges of bias and irresponsibility in the press." The idea of an annual reviewing body excited the greatest wrath, as though the quality of news and views was no business of the public. Schools of journalism, however, have helped keep the recommendation alive, and in the last few years interest in such an agency, perhaps to be appointed by the President, has been expressed both in and out of Congress. More progress perhaps would have resulted if the Commission members upon disbanding had taken steps to further the proposal, Hutchins being the only one to do so. On the other hand, Britain's Royal Commission on the Press, taking the report as a starting point, brought about in 1953 a General Council on the Press, which investigates complaints of newspaper practices. Hopefully, the last word on this side of the Atlantic has not yet been spoken.

On April 12, 1945, came the tragic news of Roosevelt's death of a cerebral hemorrhage late that afternoon in Warm Springs, Georgia, and a surge of grief encircled the globe. He had served hardly three months of his fourth term; the war was still raging; and the conditions of peace, in which he was so vitally interested, remained to be formulated. I was dining with the Nieman Fellows at the *Christian Science Monitor* building in Boston when the editor, Erwin Canham, was called aside for a moment and then announced in stricken tones, "The President has died." We looked at each other in mute dismay, for Roosevelt's magnetic personality had made us feel we had each lost a near and dear friend. How profoundly Canham himself was moved was revealed by the fact that he had failed to say, as a Christian Scientist should have, "The President has passed on."

The new executive, Harry S. Truman, was pretty much an unknown quantity, and his early acts afforded little assurance that he was equal to the responsibilities Fate had thrust upon him. In the autumn elections of 1946 the Republicans handily won both houses of Congress, placing in the Senate such demagogues and reactionaries as Joseph R. McCarthy of Wisconsin and William E. Jenner of Indiana. In consternation, leading liberals from all over the land, including outstanding figures in the labor movement like David Dubinsky of the International Ladies Garment Workers, founded Americans for Democratic Action, a nonpartisan body dedicated to reversing the conservative trend and excluding from membership believers in communism or any other system of totalitarianism. I attended the first convention in Philadelphia and presided over one of the sessions; but my son Arthur was much more deeply involved, so that thereafter I confined my efforts to assisting the cause locally while he continued active in the national field.

The Massachusetts Independent Voters Association, which has been re-established with every presidential race since Al Smith's in 1928, had taken on permanent form after 1944. We felt that a liberal movement, to exert maximum influence, should not go to sleep for four years at a stretch. Now the MIVA converted itself into a chapter of ADA in order to be able to work with a centralized organization and with kindred groups in other states; and I became the first chairman. The 1948 campaign posed our first real test. As the contest got under way, the two state-wide labor bodies, the American Federation of Labor and the Congress of Industrial Organizations, were induced to join ADA in forming the Massachusetts United Labor Committee for collective political action. They had hitherto distrusted and fought each other, and the overture would probably not have succeeded except for the fact that they were confronted with the adoption of some anti-union referenda in the election; two years before, working separately, they had failed to defeat a milder measure. At our organization meeting, however, neither group proved willing to have a member of the other serve as chairman, with the un-expected result that I found myself in that position. Before long, though, they forgot their former animosities and strove singlemindedly in the common effort.

These activities consisted in gaining votes for the national and state Democratic tickets as well as against the obnoxious referenda. Truman had been unenthusiastically nominated to succeed himself by his party and quite as unenthusiastically endorsed by the national ADA, but for progressives the Re-publican contender, Dewey, was no acceptable alternative. In retrospect it is evident that the failures of Truman's domestic program had unduly diminished his stature in liberal eyes,

for in the international sphere he had in the last two years of
his administration displayed farseeing statesmanship in such
historic acts as the Truman Doctrine for Greece and Turkey,
the Marshall Plan, and the Berlin airlift. The United Labor
Committee neglected no opportunity to advance the cause,
conducting registration drives, organizing meetings and radio
programs, issuing pamphlets and fliers, and providing sound
trucks, posters, lapel buttons, and stickers. Nationally, however, Truman's defeat seemed foredoomed—until in due
course the people recorded their will. Then to his victorious
margin of fourteen electoral votes Massachusetts contributed
an indispensable sixteen. It also elected the Democratic state
ticket and overwhelmingly rejected the anti-union referenda.

Truman's second term gave abundant evidence of the vision
and leadership which, added to his earlier accomplishments,
made seventy-five historians later rate him with the near-great
Presidents. He launched the Point Four program for underdeveloped countries, initiated the North Atlantic Defense
Treaty, and led the United States into the Korean War in support of the United Nations. This last move unexpectedly involved him in a dramatic assertion of the civil over the military power. When General Douglas MacArthur, the Korean
field commander, publicly assailed the administration's policy
of keeping the struggle a limited one, the President, other
methods failing, dismissed him on April 11, 1951, for insub-
ordination, thereby arousing intense popular excitement both
pro and con. Meanwhile, less to Truman's credit, the public
learned of petty grafters in federal positions, some of whom
enjoyed ready access to the White House; and though no
one doubted Truman's own integrity, even his well-wishers
deplored his complaisant attitude toward the culprits. Cou-
pling these two matters in a letter, I wrote the President,

I believe that the sober second thought of your critics will thoroughly justify your courageous action in removing General Mac-
Arthur from his Far Eastern duties. We who have supported you

in this and so many other measures hope that you will now display equal vigor in ridding your civilian administration of members who have been recreant to their public responsibilities.

In the hope that he would actually see the letter, it was sent in care of Dave Niles, who had continued as a presidential aide after Roosevelt's death. Truman never replied, and I do not know that it ever came to his notice.

About a month afterward, when in Washington, I discussed Truman's strange tolerance of venal officials with W. Averell Harriman, his special assistant on foreign affairs. He no doubt rightly attributed it to a defect of his virtues: a blind loyalty to friends. The President, Harriman said, had himself been so often and so unfairly attacked as to be loath to think ill of those now under fire. "What he doesn't realize is that the American people regard the White House as a national shrine which must not be sullied by even the appearance of any misdoing." Later in the day I saw Truman in action at a press conference, this at the very time General MacArthur was venting his woes to a Senate committee. Meeting him afterward I congratulated him on his flaying of MacArthur in a recent radio broadcast, whereupon he snorted,

I only stated the facts. It was time for the President of the United States to say something to offset the big build-up Congressional committees have been giving a disobedient general. I've had trouble with him for three years. He was over there so long that he thought he had acquired a Japanese crown. If one of his sergeants or captains had acted as he has, the poor fellow wouldn't have lasted a day.

The campaign of 1952 gave Elizabeth and me our first opportunity to attend the political conventions via television. We had bought the set the year before, and it was still such a novelty in Harvard circles that faculty friends crowded around the little screen with us. Adlai E. Stevenson's nomination by the Democrats made a particular appeal to academics. Here was a man much as they fancied themselves to be—reflective, humane, undoctrinaire, highly literate, mindful more of the next generation than of the next election—with the added recommendation of having been a successful governor of a populous state. Opposing him was a great war hero with no political experience, and I for one had long been telling students that since the unthinking days of Zachary Taylor and U. S. Grant the electorate had become too sophisticated to consider military laurels a sufficient qualification for the presidency. On the initiative of Walter Johnson of the University of Chicago I joined with him and other American historians in publicly endorsing Stevenson, and locally, as chairman of the United Labor Committee, I seconded his interests. My closest tie with the presidential race, however, was through Arthur, who belonged to Stevenson's campaign staff and accompanied him on some of his trips. It was not till after the election that I myself met him.

I further assisted in a national fund-raising effort to rid the United States Senate of a pair of objectionable members. Two years before, Wisconsin's Joe McCarthy had begun his campaign of character assassination, charging worthy public officials with disloyalty and accusing even the State Department of harboring Communists; and in Indiana's Jenner he had a faithful echo. At the instance of the undergraduate Harvard Liberal Union, Mark DeWolfe Howe of the Law School, Archibald MacLeish, now of the English Department, and I signed a letter to 5,000 colleagues across the land, inviting contributions to help defeat the two undesirables and to re-elect William Benton of Connecticut, an outspoken Senate foe of McCarthyism. The Associated Press, learning of the appeal, spread word of it far and wide beyond the intended recipients. Responses poured in from all parts of the United States and all degrees of people—farmers, housewives, schoolteachers, laboring men, professors, lawyers, and doctors. The writers invariably expressed outrage at the terroristic methods, but also betrayed a state of fear and panic shocking in a free society. This is a page of recent American history one would like to forget. Some asked that their names be kept secret; others, to play safe, sent in paper money anonymously. A storekeeper wrote from York, Pa.,

Although I am not a coward, there are certain connections I have in Wisconsin which require that no publicity be given this donation except any legal report which you must file . . . and in that event I ask that it be listed as a donation with as little identification as possible.

Significantly, after each of McCarthy's two campaign radio broadcasts, the receipts took a jump. Following his second speech a District of Columbia woman wrote,

For as long as support against McCarthyism is needed, I should like to send you a monthly contribution—and I daresay many other housewives would be glad to contribute $5 or so of their house-keeping money on a regular basis, too.

The most moving incident occurred when an Italian workman in Cambridge, haunted by memories of Fascism, called at my door and against my advice handed over a legacy of $450 which he had been saving toward the purchase of a home; a few days later he returned with some cash he had solicited from friends. In all, we collected over $15,000 from 1,500 in-dividuals. Not a large sum in itself, it was, as all three of the candidates assured us, a much needed supplement to what they had obtained from other sources. After the election I ac-cepted an invitation to join the National Committee for an Effective Congress in New York, which had defrayed the over-head expenses of these activities, and have continued a mem-ber of this nonpartisan liberal organization ever since.

When the ballots were counted, Eisenhower, it hardly need be said, swept the nation, including Massachusetts, and also carried with him all the Senatorial candidates we had raised money to defeat. Locally the only gleam of comfort was the elevation to the Senate of a slim, well-set-up young man named John F. Kennedy, but even he had disappointed liberal expectations by ignoring the issue of McCarthyism in his campaign. Closely following this lone victory, moreover, came an additional bad omen for the future: the dissolution of the United Labor Committee.

Four years as its chairman had proved an enlightening experience, exciting great respect for the AFL and CIO representatives. With few exceptions they sought the welfare of society at large as well as that of wage earners, holding the two to be inseparably linked even in such peripheral concerns as civil liberties and civil rights. Moreover, they had instanced once more that men may be intelligent, well-informed, and responsible with little formal education. What I had not expected was that some of the leaders were college graduates, a fact early apparent when an AFL official complimented me on being "a good catalyst," a word rarely in my own vocabulary. I also learned at first hand how greatly the conditions and the psychology of the labor movement had changed since the bitter struggles for survival around the turn of the century. Now no one ever spoke of the "working class." They did not consider themselves apart from, but a full part of, the community. Had they thought in social categories at all, they would have declared, correctly, in view of their rise in economic status, that they, like most of us, belonged to the middle class. The rock on which the United Labor Committee split was ADA's refusal to concur with the two other groups in backing for re-election the Democratic governor, Paul A. Dever, a decision I had resisted in the ADA State Board as based on insufficient grounds. Consequently the Committee had functioned unitedly only in support of the national candidates, and the resentment of the AFL and CIO members became permanent when Dever suffered defeat. Though the three-way alliance thus came to an end, the habit of working together had taught the labor elements lessons in political cooperation which stood them in good stead when the national merger of the AFL and CIO welded them into a single state organization later in the decade. ADA, for its part, learned the hard way to rest its endorsements thereafter upon more careful study.

Nine months before the election, in February, 1952, President Truman had appointed me to the National Historical Publications Commission, a body of eleven scholars and federal officials which meets periodically in Washington to consider plans for documentary publications by public and private agencies. Frankfurter, representing the Supreme Court, was one of the group, and this enabled me to see him again with some regularity. The Commission formulated a program for bringing out under its own auspices source accounts of the ratification of the Constitution and the Bill of Rights and of the work of the First Congress, and listed for possible outside editing and financing the papers of some 300 individuals who from colonial days on had contributed vitally to the building of American civilization.

In November, 1954, eight of us on behalf of the Commission secured an appointment with President Eisenhower to present the recommendations. Appearing on the dot, we had to wait twenty minutes in an anteroom until Secretary of State Dulles left him; but, whatever problems of international moment had prolonged their conference, the President was utterly relaxed and spoiling for a chat. Without inquiring about our errand he remarked that he had always loved history, referring with particular pride to having in the final days of the war obtained for the National Archives Adolf Hitler's last will and testament. There could be no doubt of its authenticity, he said, because—unaware apparently that it could have been submitted to accredited scholars for examination—he had had it verified by J. Edgar Hoover, the FBI director. When the head of the Eisenhower Museum in Abilene had reproached him for not depositing the paper there, he had replied, "Oh hell, that happened before there was any thought of such a place." Our chairman, Wayne C. Grover, finally succeeded in passing him our report with the observation, which manifestly relieved the President, that the 106 printed pages had for his convenience been reduced to a typewritten sheet. He then shook hands all around and remarked jocularly as we went out, "I hope there is nothing you've put there that a good Republican could not approve." That has been my only meeting with this friendly, approachable man. The next year my term on the Commission expired and was not renewed. If my politics was responsible, it seemed an excessive display of partisanship, since the members have no concern with the contemporary scene, nor do they draw salaries that the faithful might have coveted.

These nonacademic interests over three decades deserve recall chiefly as reflecting the reactions of a single individual to a momentous era in our history. My participation, which was no more than that of a concerned citizen, obviously never had a determining influence.

IX

Journeys Abroad

We made our first trip overseas after nine years in Cambridge. As a student unconcerned with United States diplomatic history I had not felt the need; all my key research materials lay within the country. Only gradually did it dawn on me that I could better understand the multiple forces which had contributed to the forming of American society from a firsthand knowledge of other national cultures. This would enable me to view an accustomed way of life from the outside, be a safeguard against provincialism. My sons, too, were reaching an age when foreign travel would be profitable, and Elizabeth would realize a long-cherished desire.

A combination of circumstances brought these considerations to a head. One was an invitation to deliver a series of public lectures at the University College of the University of London and repeat them at the University of Edinburgh. The time fortunately coincided with an impending leave of absence from Harvard as well as with a lull in the editing of the *History of American Life*. Arthur, moreover, who would graduate from Phillips Exeter in June, 1933, at fifteen and a half, could well afford to wait a year before entering college, while active-minded Tom, though only eleven, would also benefit from the experience. To make the most of the undertaking Elizabeth and I decided to approach England from the east instead of the west—via the Pacific and Asia. This was before the day of long-distance air travel, but in any event we would have preferred the more leisurely means of steamer and train. When we arranged for passports, Arthur asked that his middle name appear as Meier instead of Bancroft, so as thereafter to be known as Junior, and this we acceded to without foreseeing the confusion that would arise when in due course he adopted his father's profession and taught at the same university.

We set out on September 2, 1933, from Montreal by rail for Vancouver, our port of sailing. The Great Depression, then in its fourth year, showed little sign of abating, and a few nights before in Cambridge a visitor from Washington at Felix Frankfurter's had indeed advised us not to go, on the ground that the United States might well collapse before our return. We had taken the precaution of defraying in advance all the basic charges of the trip through Thomas Cook & Son in Boston, so that the declining foreign-exchange rate affected only minor expenses. How different matters might have been appears in the fact that in Bangkok, for example, the English pound stood at $5.61 instead of the normal $4.89. The economic shadows probably explain why we encountered so few fellow countrymen in the Far East. By the time we reached Europe, however, the situation had bettered with the improvement of conditions at home.

We made the two weeks' crossing of the Pacific from Vancouver on the luxury liner *Empress of Japan*, docking at Honolulu long enough for a quick view of the city and its environs, including the naval base at Pearl Harbor, as yet unknown to history. An unexpected fellow passenger was the Japanese Yusuke Tsurumi, to whom Charles A. Beard had given me a letter for presentation in Tokyo. When I made myself known, Tsurumi moved his deck chair beside ours, and we immediately struck up a friendship. An urbane, sophisticated man who spoke English fluently and had often lectured in the United States, Tsurumi was in his own country a liberal member of the lower house of the Diet as well as a best-selling novelist. On reaching Tokyo he opened doors for us which as mere tourists we could not otherwise have entered.

Through his good offices, for instance, I conferred with the leading members of the Cabinet, each of whom voiced an earnest desire for what one called "unclouded skies with the United States," while at the same time defending Japan's recent conquest of Manchuria as a benefit to the inhabitants. Though the government had by then served notice on the League of Nations of its intention to withdraw, Prime Minister Saito said with some emotion, "Japan cannot live apart from the world politically. I do not wish my country to abandon the League." Indeed, Nagai, the Minister of Overseas Affairs, wore a Lincoln penny as a watch charm, explaining that it was out of admiration for the famous American and because the accompanying words "Liberty" and "In God We Trust" expressed the guiding principles of all great statesmanship. Subsequent developments indicate that these personages, if speaking truthfully, were unable to breast the powerful influence of the country's army and navy elements. This appears unquestionably to have been so in the case of Prince Konoye, president of the upper chamber of the Diet, who with his lovely Princess entertained our family one day at luncheon. As Prime Minister on the eve of Pearl Harbor he resisted to nearly the last the launching of the attack. Most of the conversations required an interpreter—"interrupter"—though I sensed that some of the officials understood English even if they did not or would not speak it.

We, of course, did the usual sightseeing in and out of Tokyo, visiting Nikko, Kyoto, and other places and being enchanted on every hand with the well-preserved memorials of bygone days and the neatness and beauty of the landscape. For one day and night as guests of a Shinto sect at Nara we lived native-fashion, wearing kimonos, going about in *zori* (grass sandals) indoors, and squatting on the floor upon which we later slept. As an over-all impression of the country I wrote in my journal:

The American tourist naturally prefers the older, passing Japan. Most Japanese, on the other hand, boast of the prevalence of European conveniences of living. They like to think of themselves, along with the United States and Russia, as being an up-and-coming people imbued with the spirit of youth and hope and energy. From earliest times they have adapted and assimilated foreign cultures, notably the Chinese and Indian. The Occidentalization of Japan is thus not a new phenomenon. I hope they won't pay too high a price for it, however.

Looking ahead, let me say something of my subsequent dis-illusionment with Tsurumi. On his journeys to America after our return we saw a good deal of him in Cambridge. In fact he placed his son Shunsuke—now a distinguished Japanese professor of philosophy—in my charge while he studied a year at a preparatory school and then at Harvard. In these visits Tsurumi betrayed a growing admiration of Hitler in bald con-trast to his former democratic professions. Then, after the war broke out, he delivered a radio broadcast in Tokyo, monitored in Washington by the Federal Communications Commission, in which he flayed the Americans as "barbaric" and "brutal" but basically weaklings who, having brought about the strug-gle, would soon yield to superior Japanese might. I, of course, had expected him to side with his country but not to go out of his way to traduce a people whom he had known so well at first hand. When he came back to the United States a few years after the peace, he tried repeatedly to see me, but I had no heart for renewing our relations.

Leaving Japan for Peking by way of Tangku, we arrived at the North China seaport late in the evening and became im-mediately conscious of the proximity of Japanese invading forces. The floor of the railway station for our inland destination was crowded with sleeping Chinese soldiers, a foretaste of the embattled atmosphere of Peking itself. Soldiers strode its streets and closely guarded its gates, which no one could enter or leave without authorization. From a sightseer's point of view the great rabbit warren of humanity, though still a joy, was largely a city of faded glories, the resplendent architectural survivals being studiously neglected by the current "emancipated" generation. For example, weeds and bushes disfigured the tiers of blue-tiled roofs of the exquisite Temple of Heaven. Outside the city we visited the Great Wall of China some fifty miles away, going by train as far as the Nankou Pass (through which Marco Polo had reached the Celestial Kingdom), then being conveyed the remaining few miles by basket carriers. To see the stupendous stone python winding and twisting over the mountains was like being transported to a hardly credible past. Close at hand, but still outside Peking's walls, lay Yenching and Tsing Hua Universities on adjoining campuses. The historians there extended a cordial welcome, and I met a future colleague in John K. Fairbank, who, accompanied by his talented bride, Wilma, was improving his knowledge of the Chinese language. He was later to develop instruction in Far Eastern history at Harvard.

Heading southward, we next stopped briefly at Nanking, the national capital, then continued to Shanghai, where Pingchia Kuo, today a professor at Southern Illinois University, guided our tour of the sprawling city. A quite recent Harvard Ph.D. in history, he had made the three-day journey down the Yangtse from his teaching post at the National Wuhan University for the purpose. Whole blocks of the westernized business section, including the country's largest printing plant, still lay in ruins from Japanese bombing the year before. With Manchuria lost, one wondered how long China proper could retain its independence. To reach Hong Kong we had to go by sea in the absence then of rail connections. The situation of the tiny British possession was unlike that of any other city we saw in the Orient, rising sharply from a narrow plain at the water's edge up the side of a small mountain, with the streets paralleling one another at different levels, and the whole gleaming at night like a gigantic Christmas tree.

Apart from its own attractions Hong Kong provided a point of departure for two side expeditions. One was up the Pearl River by a puffing little boat to Canton, the metropolis of South China. To recur to my journal:

It affords an even greater impression of higgledy-piggledy streets, social chaos and indescribable smells than Peking. . . . Nor have we elsewhere seen such brilliance of color, the store fronts exhibiting every hue of the rainbow. Only one other aspect exceeds the panorama of the streets. This is the teeming life on the many canals and the river, every stretch dotted with sampans and other varieties of houseboats, on which parents with their numerous young eke out an existence amid cats, dogs and chickens, cooking and washing in the filthy water.

There were, in addition, of course, gorgeous temples and similar tourist magnets, but it was the spectacle of the common life that has etched the deepest memory.

The other trip was to the Philippines, of special interest at the time to an American historian because this far-off dependency of the United States was in the throes of achieving national freedom. Thanks to a letter from Dave Niles, Governor General Frank Murphy put himself, his aides, and his official car at our disposal, so that there was little in or about Manila we missed. Some months before, Congress had adopted a plan for the country's independence, subject to Filipino approval, with the consummation to come in 1946, after which the United States would retain some army and navy bases. Murphy made it possible for me to talk with the two native leaders, each with a large popular following, who held opposing views on the military provisions. Sergio Osmeña, his round face and soft voice suggesting his Chinese lineage, explained that he advocated acceptance as the best arrangement feasible; but Manuel Quezon heatedly cried, "How can we really be free while your guns frown down on us? We would have responsibility without authority." His sharp features and fiery manner reflected his Spanish blood. I gathered, however, that despite his show of passion he was primarily engaged in shadowboxing with Osmeña for political advantage. In due course the Philippine legislature did in fact reject Congress's offer and secured new terms whereby the army posts were to be abandoned and the question of naval stations left to future negotiation.

Murphy, who had resigned his position as an outstanding reform mayor of Detroit to go to the islands as a Roosevelt appointee, spoke with just pride of having introduced playgrounds in Manila, as well as juvenile courts, the indeterminate sentence for criminals, and other features of social progressivism at home. But, as I wrote Niles, "I sense that he feels he is out of the main current of national affairs and, subconsciously, is growing discontented." He was not destined to remain so long, however. Elected governor of Michigan three years later, he was by 1939 Roosevelt's Attorney General and the next year a Justice of the Supreme Court.

In all we spent about four weeks on the Chinese mainland, and though we observed only the more westernized parts, certain reactions were unavoidable. Our chief feeling of depression arose from the almost universal ignorance, poverty, and miserable plane of living of the people. Governmentally, too, the country seemed hopeless, being run by corrupt men who showed no concern for promoting the general welfare. The Chinese intellectuals with whom I talked, many of them trained in the United States, agreed that unless the Nationalist regime moved rapidly to improve the lot of the masses communism was bound to take over. And clearly some of them considered that this would be the lesser of the evils.

Bidding good-by to Hong Kong for the last time, we sailed

for what was then French Indochina but today consists of North and South Vietnam, Cambodia, and Laos, four countries which are tinderboxes of conflict. Landing at Saigon on November 10, we witnessed after dark a great parade of natives with torches, colorful floats, and giant images of dragons and other mythological creatures, all designed to commemorate the eve of Armistice Day. It was strange to see Asians celebrating an event which they had shared only vicariously and which had brought their own land no benefit. Our prime objective, however, was Angkor, 360 miles in the interior, the site of the ancient Khmer civilization which had mysteriously vanished after flourishing from the ninth to the thirteenth century. This required a two-day auto trip. The huge stone fortresses, gateways, towers, and temples, which the French authorities had retrieved from the encroaching jungle, had been erected by a people ignorant of the function of the keystone in constructing an arch, but who notwithstanding had built massively with richly decorated bas-relief walls and innumerable figures of Buddha. In the country about were elephants and monkeys, and turbaned guards with rifles patrolled our sleeping quarters in the hotel courtyard by night to ward off prowling tigers.

From Angkor we motored to the Siamese frontier to board a train for Bangkok, the center of another strange world but in this case inhabited by the living. Interlaced with *klongs* (canals) and studded with varicolored, multispired temples, the city presented to Occidental eyes a fairyland effect. Though it lay under martial law due to an abortive revolution a few weeks before, fortunately this in no way interfered with our own movements. That Bangkok, despite all evidence to the contrary, was waking to the present became evident upon encountering an American who was manager of the King's expanding cinema enterprises.

The next ports of call were Penang, an enchanting tropical island off the Malay Peninsula, and Rangoon, the capital of

Burma, followed by three weeks in India. Entering at Calcutta, we crossed to Bombay with stopovers at Benares, Agra, Delhi (where we attended a session of the legislature), Jaipur, and Udaipur, plus a side trip from Calcutta to Darjeeling in the Himalayas for a sunrise view of Mt. Kinchinjunga. What struck us most forcibly about the great subcontinent was the juxtaposition of rags and riches: the squalor of the bulk of the population as contrasted, on the one hand, with the sprinkling of fine modern cities and, on the other, with the reminders of a past typified by such displays of luxury and taste as Agra Fort, the Taj Mahal, and Amber. A few of these the British had restored to their original state.

India brought to sharp focus certain reflections regarding the Western impact on Asia. Tsurumi had remarked that the Christian missionaries, though highminded and dedicated, had not usually been people qualified to transmit to Orientals the cultural and intellectual values of the Occident; and aside from occasional medical missionaries, that too was our impression. Nor had the long years of European imperialism accomplished much more, for this interposition had consisted mainly of exploitation by force with scant regard for what Kipling had called "the white man's burden" of bettering the common lot. The British, for instance, had established some universities in India, but had done little or nothing to provide lower schools or to introduce improved sanitation or modern agriculture. A British colonial official had even refused to tell us the Hindustani equivalent for "Thank you," declaring, "No white person ever thanks an Indian for anything." Nor had the example of cleanliness and civic enterprise in centers like Shanghai and Bombay altered rooted customs of the native inhabitants, let alone of those outside. From hindsight it is obvious that I did not give due weight to the training the British gave the Indians in the civil service, which was to stand the country in such good stead when it won freedom. Except for the United

States in the Philippines, however, no other foreign government discharged this function.

Christmas Day, unlike any other in our experience, saw us in thin summer clothing voyaging under a blazing sun through the Arabian Sea toward Cairo via the sand-bordered Suez Canal, arriving on New Year's Day, 1934, with no letup in the heat. During two weeks in Egypt we again observed the remains of a lost civilization against the ugly reality of widespread human degradation. Our itinerary included, besides Cairo and the neighboring Great Pyramids, a rail journey up the Nile to Aswan and Luxor (where we inspected the recently excavated tomb of King Tutankhamen). Then embarking at Alexandria, we crossed the Mediterranean to Piraeus.

Had we approached Greece by way of Western Europe, the novel aspects of its life would doubtless have appeared more striking, but after the exotic lands we had seen, the people and their ways seemed not unlike what we had always known. The Acropolis and the other Athenian vestiges of classical times surpassed our highest expectations, and in this instance there were no offsetting scenes of social misery. We also visited Mycenae and in Old Corinth examined the diggings of the American School of Classical Studies. Then by Mediterranean steamer we continued to Marseilles, stopping in transit at Naples to view the city and the ruins of Pompeii. Proceeding by rail through France to Boulogne, we arrived by channel boat at Folkestone, England, on January 31. Approximately five months had elapsed since setting out and ill health had not held us up a single day.

The next four months we spent in Britain, chiefly in London, dwelling in an old-fashioned—but furnace-heated—lodging house in Bloomsbury near the British Museum. Freed from the tyranny of a timetable, we took our pleasures leisurely, exploring every part of the city by foot or bus or the Underground. Hyde Park on Sunday afternoons offered a ceaseless attraction, for one never knew what outlandish political or economic doctrines the speakers might expound. Once a great procession of striking miners from Wales converged on the area, but all our fears of violence vanished when the band began blaring, and the marchers singing, not the "Internationale" but "Way Down upon the Swanee River." We also attended the theater, being especially charmed by Elisabeth Bergner in *Escape Me Never*. Through the good offices of Harold Laski of the London School of Economics and Denis W. Brogan, a former Harvard graduate student then teaching at the University College of London and now at Cambridge University, I soon came to know various English historians, G. P. Gooch, R. H. Tawney, and A. F. Pollard among others. Harold was the same sparkling conversationalist of old, addicted to the same extravagant statements and darkly predicting that the British masses, though congenitally averse to bloodshed, would in their wrath and despair take power by force in order to right their wrongs at the hands of the class-ridden Tory government.

My lectures at the University College, starting in mid-February and open to the public, continued for four weeks at the rate of two a week. Beginning on a facetious note, I observed that apart from Oxford and London no English universities offered instruction in American history, apparently in the belief that the United States was too young to have a history, whereas I had just come from a region of the globe so ancient as to think Britain itself had none. The series was based on the formula of *New Viewpoints in American History*, treating certain significant themes genetically under the inclusive title of "Social Forces in American History." These embraced such aspects as "The Development of American Nationality," "The Old South: A Variant Culture," and "The American Way of Life." The audiences, to my disappointment, appeared to contain more Americans than subjects of George V. There was little in the climate of opinion at the time to foreshadow the great surge of interest in the teaching and writing of United

States history that was to follow World War II. It was in this later era that Arthur, Jr., then a Harvard professor, delivered a group of addresses on American history at the University College in the very same series, exactly twenty-five years after listening as a lad of sixteen to his father. Invitations to speak also took me to the University of Liverpool and the University of South Wales.

En route to the University of Edinburgh, where I was to repeat the London talks, we stopped off as a matter of course at Cambridge to see the place from which our home town had taken its name and the college which had nurtured John Harvard. Edinburgh, with its main thoroughfare overtopped by an ancient castle, had a special Old World flavor; the faculty community was most cordial; and the lectures created more general interest than in London, perhaps because of the fewer counter attractions. We thoroughly enjoyed, too, the crusty old ladies at our lodging house, who were fiercely anti-English until they thought one day I had belittled the Queen, when they became just as fiercely pro-English. By bus we also went to Sir Walter Scott's Abbotsford and the Trossachs and spent a day at St. Andrews University. Returning to London in mid-May through the Lake district, the countryside brilliant with buttercups, we visited Stratford-on-Avon (attending a performance of *Henry V*) and Oxford University with its famous Bodleian Library. Felix Frankfurter, the Eastman professor at Oxford that year, lent our stay a personal touch.

The last two months took us to the Continent—to Paris, Switzerland, northern and central Italy, Vienna, Prague, Saxony, Bavaria, plus a Rhine trip from Wiesbaden to Cologne, and a final stop in Brussels—dutifully viewing the sights as enjoined by Baedeker. In Germany, where Hitler had seized power the year before, portents of the ugly times to come were already disturbingly visible. This I had had a foretaste of while crossing the Pacific, in a conversation with the Nazi ambassador to Japan, then proceeding to Tokyo. When I spoke of Carl

Schurz as having been one of America's great public servants, Herr Voretsch curtly termed him "a traitor to German ideals" and denounced all popular government as "criminal folly." "A country should be governed by authority, not by majority," he declaimed. And to these sentiments he callously added a forthright vindication of Hitler's anti-Semitic persecutions. In the *Vaterland* itself we saw placards reading NO JEWS ADMITTED, and in the great square of Nuremberg one night we witnessed a Nazi rally at which the violent oratory, backed by the disciplined response of the crowd, sent chills down our spines.

Reaching American soil again by the end of August, we could look back upon a fruitful and memorable year, one which had broadened our intellectual as well as our geographical horizons. In a sense, moreover, we were able to relive the experience that first year at home, for Elizabeth and Arthur had also kept journals, and every week we read to one another what had befallen the family just twelve months before. It was an illuminating demonstration of the nature of firsthand historical evidence, since each of us had recorded those things which had seemed most worth while and sometimes these greatly differed.

Five years later, on August 16, 1939, Elizabeth and I took a shorter jaunt out of the country, this time a fortnight's cruise in the West Indies to celebrate our approaching twenty-fifth wedding anniversary. The American tropics proved hardly less fascinating than the Asian, but in a different way, since the people were far more westernized and there were no remains of dead civilizations where we touched land. In listening to the crisp accents of the Negroes in English Jamaica the thought occurred to me that the Negroes in the southern United States, contrary to the common view, had probably derived their drawl from association with the whites rather than the reverse. In Colombia, where the Spanish influence predominated, we visited Barranquilla and Cartagena, the latter still possessing crumbling town walls of Spanish days. Our final call was at the Panama Canal, an engineering feat which far surpassed that of the Suez Canal. In planning the excursion we had as a matter of political principle rejected the superior inducements of a German-owned line in favor of a United Fruit Company ship under the American flag; before the end of the voyage we felt that virtue had been rewarded. The imminence of the outbreak of war caused the Nazi vessel in alarm to dump its passengers summarily in Havana, compelling them to find their way home as best they could.

Our second extensive absence from the United States resulted from an invitation of a visiting professorship at the University of Leyden during the academic year 1948-49. I readily accepted, for, as in England fifteen years before, American history received little or no attention in Dutch academic institutions. Moreover, Elizabeth and I would have an opportunity, denied in our world tour, of dwelling long enough in a foreign country to feel in some measure a part of it. In addition to generous living arrangements, the terms included the use of a Ford car. On September 24, 1948, we sailed from Hoboken on the *Nieuw Amsterdam* as guests of the Holland-America line.

What we had expected to find in the Netherlands was unconsciously fashioned by childhood reading of Mary Mapes Dodge's *Hans Brinker*—a story, incidentally, little known there —and this to a degree proved true, though of course modern ways predominated. Dikes and canals interspersed the landscape, and in quiet fishing villages the people continued to wear quaint peasant costumes and wooden shoes. Shadowing both the old and the new, however, were the effects of the long Nazi occupation, ended but three years before. Strewn along the beaches at quarter-mile intervals still stood massive concrete German pillboxes erected to resist possible Allied invasion from across the North Sea, and nearly everybody had harrowing tales to tell of the grim days. Virtually all the professors we met had been either internees because of suspected underground activities or hostages for the good conduct of others, or had fled under assumed names to the countryside to escape arrest. The entire Leyden faculty had quit in 1940 in protest against the dismissal of some Jewish colleagues, and the classrooms remained closed throughout the occupation. Peace, too, had brought its problems in a badly deranged economic system, difficulties further aggravated by the revolution for independence in Indonesia, which had long constituted a major source of national wealth and employment. But for America's Marshall Plan, which went into effect just as we arrived, the outlook would have been unrelievedly bleak.

We had hoped to reside close by the University, but the housing shortage prevented this, and the Dutch Foreign Office secured us accommodations in the Kasteel Oud-Wassenaar —the Castle of Old Wassenaar—seven miles from Leyden and three from The Hague. Our Ford of course made the arrangement entirely feasible. The onetime mansion of a tycoon who had amassed his fortune in Indonesia, the so-called Kasteel was a many-turreted brick building in Victorian style, to which a large wing had been added to convert it into a hotel. Set in a great wooded estate bordered by trim flower beds and holly trees, it fronted picturesquely on a pond inhabited by swans and ducks. The guests were of many nationalities including some Dutch. A fellow American, with whom I took Sunday-morning walks, was Alan Valentine, president on leave from the University of Rochester, who a few months before had awarded me an honorary degree. He was the administrator of the Marshall Plan in Holland and gave me an insight into the country's economic plight which would otherwise have been unobtainable.

The city of Leyden is in its older parts still definitely a medieval town. The buildings mellowed with age hug the streets, the streets themselves are narrow, winding, and sunless, and the intersecting canals sluggish and unfenced, the whole conveying an atmosphere of antique charm. The University,

founded by William the Silent in 1585 and government-sup-
ported, continues to conduct classes in some of the ancient
halls, including the one where I held forth. The prior preparation of the boys and girls consists of a rigorous training in the
secondary schools which carries them a year or more beyond
the point reached at that stage in the United States. At the
University, however, they undergo a sea change. For the first
year or so they generally loaf or play. This, I was informed,
allows them to recuperate from the unrelieved grind they had
earlier endured and to indulge extracurricular interests which
they then had no opportunity for. The custom accords with a
faculty program which prescribes no course examinations and
permits the students to take as long a time as they wish to
graduate. When ready, they merely present themselves for a
set of comprehensive examinations in their major subjects.

Also different from the American system, the undergraduates upon entering the institution at once enroll in a professional school—Law, Science, Medicine, and the like. As a
postwar development, however, the University also offered
a group of courses of broader character (known as the *Studium Generale* or General Studies), which, though leading
to no degree, nonetheless attracted a considerable following.
Apart from this provision the closest to a liberal-arts curriculum was that of the Faculty of Letters and Philosophy, with
which I was affiliated, but to an American its offerings were
sadly deficient. The social sciences were represented by a
single professor of economics, a half-time professor of sociology (a subject newly introduced that year), none at all
in political science, and but two in the whole sweep of history. Of these last, one taught only the Netherlands past,
while the other divided himself between modern Russian
history and the evolution of the idea of nationality, leaving
untouched the huge gaps in between.

As I was expected to deliver an inaugural address, I had
spent part of the summer writing it and at the same time

studied the Dutch language notwithstanding the assurance that everyone in the faculty and the student body knew English. In fact, this also proved true of tradesfolk and most others we encountered. If they had not learned it in school, they had picked it up from British and Canadian soldiers during the war or by listening to the BBC. Consequently my halting Dutch was of little use, since people generally preferred to practice up on their acquired tongue.

My address portrayed the historical forces which had elevated America from a colonial status to its current position of global leadership. The exercises, marked by pomp and circumstance in the Dutch academic tradition, started at four in the afternoon, I being somewhat self-consciously arrayed in cap, gown, and hood over a dress suit. For what took place let me call on my diary:

The Rector Magnificus opened the proceedings with complimentary remarks to the visiting professor in the presence of the faculty assembled in the Senaatskamer, after which we marched to the nearby Groot-Auditorium, preceded by two attendants bearing maces. Here, from a lofty rostrum, I read my speech on "The Rise of the United States as a World Power." The audience filled the room and seemed attentive. Only a few went to sleep—which from my observation is a common occurrence on such occasions despite the stiff and uncomfortable seats. . . . There followed a reception which, according to custom, *we* gave to the faculty and others, including officers of the various student societies. The refreshments, in accordance with academic protocol, consisted of bouillon and port wine. To top off the day, we, as we had been directed, feasted a group of faculty dignitaries and their wives in the evening at the Gulden Vlies, the principal restaurant.

With these ceremonies disposed of, life assumed a normal tempo. I gave two courses at the university. One, a systematic account of United States history, brought in whenever possible interrelations with the Netherlands to make the subject of more interest. The other, in the *Studium Generale*, surveyed contemporary America and its problems, social, economic, and political. Desiring a wall map as a teaching aid, I discovered that the University possessed none either of the United States or even of North America, though my classroom lay within a stone's throw of where the Pilgrims had lived for twelve years and notwithstanding that Holland itself had once owned a goodly slice of the thirteen colonies. In the end I had to obtain a map from America. Another difficulty, equally unanticipated, required a different type of solution. That was the reluctance of students to ask questions or challenge statements. This, I learned upon inquiry, was the fixed Dutch attitude. As one youth said, "If a professor does not know more about his subject than we do, he would not be a professor." To pierce the barrier I set aside the last quarter of each lecture period to raise questions myself until they got used to doing so. Thereafter most of them would stay on a half-hour or so after the bell to continue the discussion. This more relaxed relationship, I suspect, led to our being invited to visit students in their rooms which, in the absence of dormitories, were tucked away in the dingy upper stories of buildings in the town. There, to the accompaniment of tea and cakes, the exchanges consisted of a free give-and-take.

From time to time I also lectured to academic and public audiences away from Leyden. Being the only American professor in Holland that year made me in repeated demand. The question most frequently asked about the United States on these occasions concerned our treatment of the Negro: how could we square this with our democratic professions? Though it was impossible then to cite or even foresee the school-desegregation decision of 1954, I endeavored to clarify the historical roots and essentially sectional character of the problem and noted the many evidences of the race's advance in human dignity and economic status in my own lifetime. At the University of Utrecht I came to know Professor Pieter Geyl, of whom I was to see more later in America. Towering in physique as well as in learning, Geyl was a somewhat controversial figure in Dutch academic circles for having pioneered a new conception of that nation's early history. Needless to say, he differed violently with John Lothrop Motley's interpretation. Because of this and his other scholarly contributions he stood in the first rank of Europe's historians. Only a few years before, he had been one of the professors interned by the Nazis, but even this ordeal had not halted his intellectual labors.

I also spoke outside Holland at the University of Louvain, a five-hour auto drive from the Kasteel Oud-Wassenaar by way of Antwerp. The unique feature of its curriculum springs from the institution's location on the linguistic boundary of Belgium, which obliges every course to be given twice, once in French and once in Flemish. Despite the fact that mine was still a third language the lectures were well attended. The Louvain Library, it will be remembered, had been leveled by German bombers during World War I and rebuilt by an outpouring of contributions from American school children and college students. During the second war its holdings were again destroyed but with the walls left standing, and this time Americans responded with quantities of books. Nearly everyone Elizabeth and I met expressed unrestrained gratitude for these acts of generosity, yet, even so, the authorities had not seen fit to introduce any instruction in American history or literature. This they might well have done on purely educational grounds considering the intrinsic and increasing importance of these subjects.

Other excursions outside the Netherlands consisted mainly of sightseeing. During the Christmas recess we revisited Paris. "Its architectural beauty," to quote from my diary, "impresses me more than it did fourteen years ago, whether in the monumental streets of the city proper or in the winding caverns of the Left Bank." By chance we dropped in one day at the Palais du Chaillot when the U.N. Security Council was debating what action to take with reference to Indonesia's struggle for independence. At the American delegation's urging, the Council called for an immediate cease-fire and the mutual surrender of political prisoners, a move adverse to Holland which created keen resentment, as we were not slow to learn upon returning there.

We spent Christmas eve in Paris with a party of Americans, the men all connected with the administering of the Marshall Plan. W. Averell Harriman, President Truman's roving ambassador for the program, described what it was accomplishing, thus supplementing what Valentine had said of its progress in Holland. When the talk turned to domestic politics, Harriman, according to my diary, "deplores Truman's tendency to make up his mind before hearing all sides of a question and thinks he needs someone like FDR had in Harry Hopkins to call, 'Whoa, wait a minute!'" It is only fair to say that two years later in Washington, when Harriman was serving as liaison officer between the White House and the State Department, he insisted I had misunderstood him, that on the contrary Truman always made a thorough study of a problem before acting, counseling with others and often reading the relevant documents far into the night. If my version be accepted, his original view doubtless reflected a widespread popular impression which a more intimate association had so completely dispelled as to make him forget he could ever have shared it.

During the long Easter vacation we traveled by plane to Copenhagen and then by boat and train to Stockholm and Oslo, places omitted in our world tour. The three Scandinavian countries presented both likenesses and differences too well known to warrant repetition here. Of professional interest was the fact that, in contrast to Leyden and Louvain, the University of Uppsala in Sweden and Norway's University of Oslo were vigorously prosecuting the study of United States history, especially America's literary contributions. At Oslo the professor in charge, Sigmund Skaard, had taken graduate work at the University of Pennsylvania. His father-in-law, Halvdan Koht, had been a treasured friend since serving as visiting professor at Harvard twenty years before. As Foreign Minister during World War II he had rejected the Nazi ultimatum for Norway's surrender and fled with his government into exile in London. Now, at the age of seventy-six, in academic retirement, he was still a veritable Viking of a man, hale, hearty, and continuing his scholarly labors. Though his field was the Norwegian past, his volume *The American Spirit in Europe*, published later that year, showed a wide-ranging and perceptive knowledge of United States history. It is still the only book on the subject.

Another trip grew out of Elizabeth's interest in the so-called skipper-schools, which offer instruction to the children of the bargemen who ceaselessly traverse the rivers and canals. Whenever a boat ties up for more than a few days, the youngsters go ashore for lessons and then, with their scholastic progress entered in their record books, resume their studies at the next stopping place. After Elizabeth visited several of the schools on her own, the Ministry of Education provided us with a car and a guide for a more extensive inspection of the institutions, including two maintained by the government in West Germany at Duisburg. Everywhere the buildings were well equipped, the teachers dedicated, and the pupils earnest and responsive. Upon our return to America Elizabeth published an account of the schools in the *Harvard Educational Review*.

A by-product of the expedition was our first sight of the Ruhr since the war. Although the fighting had ended four years before, evidences of the devastation appeared on every hand. Of Wesel and Emmerich, for instance, I said in my diary, these once thriving cities "are unbelievably and indescribably in ruins from the Allied air attacks. . . . Little has been done to remove the rubble except barely to clear the streets and sidewalks. Where an occasional room in a bombed building is habitable, there people are wretchedly living." Whether in town or country, the dearth of men was conspicuous, a grim sequel to the bloodshed. In short, we perceived no signs of the miraculous economic recovery of the years just ahead.

Our most unexpected experience in Holland was tea with Queen Juliana at her country palace at Soestdijk, two hours' drive from Wassenaar. Far from a royal command, her invitation graciously offered us a choice of either of two afternoons. Indeed, all the circumstances of the call proved delightfully informal. She received us in person, served tea and cakes with her own hands, furnished cigarettes (Lucky Strikes), chatted freely, and persuaded us to stay on longer when we first rose to leave. We had discussed in advance whether to address her as "Your Majesty," but when with her it would have seemed out of place to do so. The conversation ranged widely, as these illustrative jottings indicate:

She expressed pride in the war record of the University of Leyden, where she once studied. . . . She thinks the curriculum of the secondary schools entirely too stiff but that reform would be difficult because of internal resistance. "What we need," she said wryly, "is a mass murder of the school administrators.". . . When I spoke of Holland's bad public relations in the U.S., she said unworriedly that her country always failed at that sort of thing. . . . As a gratifying postwar development she told of the plan of associated charities making headway in some Dutch communities (and, I did not remark, common in the U.S. since the 1880's).

She even inquired about our children and our grandchildren, exclaiming "Cunning" and "Lovely" at the drawings in some children's books which Marian, Arthur's wife, had written and illustrated and which Elizabeth presented to her. As we started to go, she brought in the two youngest princesses (the elder two being on an outing with their father in Austria), and our last view was of her smiling in the doorway with one of them in her arms.

To sum up our over-all impressions of the year, we liked the Dutch. We liked their contentment with simple pleasures and their slower pace of life as compared with our high-geared land. On Sunday it seemed as though the entire population bicycled sedately through the countryside with babies peeping out from rumble seats. And they rode apparently not to arrive somewhere but to savor the joys of getting there. Special paths generally paralleled the highways for their convenience and safety. We liked their love of flowers, no house however humble being without a splash of color in the windows. By the same token we liked their sense of humor, which invariably caused them and us to chuckle and laugh at the same things. We gained some notion, too, of what it means to be a citizen of a tiny country. Educated Hollanders as a matter of course must know not only English but usually also French and German, since the people depend largely on foreign consumption of both their economic and intellectual products. As a case in point, a learned work in Dutch finds only a limited audience, but in English or some other major language it reaches a far wider and more influential readership.

We also perceived here and there among intellectuals an underlying resentment springing from Holland's decline from its once great role in the world. In the seventeenth century it had shone in philosophy, in painting, in medicine, mathematics, and astronomy, and had ruled a vast colonial empire in addition. With their eyes fixed on that golden age some Dutchmen appeared to feel a psychological need to build up their pride of nationality by demeaning the achievements of an upstart country like America. Her achievements, they observed, counted only in the material sphere. A law professor at Utrecht, for example, cursorily dismissed the Marshall Plan by saying, "You give us the money, but we will take care of the culture." In cold fact, however, we noted little evidence of creative work in literature, the drama, or the fine arts, in all of which the United States stood high, and the famed Amsterdam civic orchestra certainly seemed no better than the Boston Symphony, the New York Philharmonic, or several other American ensembles. Though often sorely tempted, we took pains not to unfurl our own flag. It was undoubtedly this feeling of inferiority that heightened the wrath toward the United States for hampering Dutch efforts to recover Indonesia.

We returned to America at the end of May, 1949, with some sense of having known intimately a foreign people as well as of having attained a fresh perspective on our native land.

X

Retirement

In the spring of 1953, when I was sixty-five, the Harvard Corporation notified me that I would reach the minimum retiring age by the end of the following academic year and invited me to remain till seventy. I had, however, for some years been looking forward to retirement. The life of a professor had been congenial and intellectually exhilarating—none in my view could have been more rewarding—but at sixty-six I would be completing forty-two years of teaching, and anything else I had worth saying could better be said in print, for which there would be more leisure. Besides, younger men were coming along with fresh insights and interests and deserved their place in the sun. As a further consideration, American social history, which had been my paramount scholarly concern, was now firmly established in colleges and universities. That battle was won. Indeed, the concept had given birth to specialized courses in the field—intellectual history, urban history, the history of science, and others—and even political history was being presented as basically an expression of social and economic forces. I therefore decided to withdraw at the earlier time.

A group of colleagues attended my last lecture in the spring of 1954, as was the custom on such occasions. Several nights later the Department gave a dinner for two members who had retired a few years before and me; and not long afterward the Nieman alumni, holding their triennial reunion, surprised me with the gift of a tape recorder. As still another farewell gesture, Kenneth Chorley, president of Colonial Williamsburg, arranged a banquet at the University Club in New York, inviting the members of the Institute of Early American History and Culture (which he regarded as my child), two of my publishers, and others, including my sons. John Krout of Columbia, a contributor to the *History of American Life*, made the principal address. Among the other speakers were Arthur and Tom, whose remarks were particularly moving. I responded with such words as I could muster, and Chorley concluded the evening by presenting me with a mahogany humidor made out of a replica of a colonial tea canister and bearing a brass plate inscribed "Scholar, Teacher, Counselor." It was a strictly stag affair, but Mrs. Chorley compensated for this in Elizabeth's case by entertaining her at dinner and the theater, and Chorley himself added a gift of a set of dinner plates modeled on those used in Williamsburg in the eighteenth century.

In my three decades the faces in the Harvard History Department had completely altered. Of the senior members at the beginning all had died except McIlwain and Haring, and they, though still living in the community, were no longer teaching. Morison, a somewhat later comer, and Merk, who had long since risen to full rank, reached the minimum retirement age at the same time as I; but Sam chose to continue another year and Fred for two. In the thirty years, too, the size of the teaching staff had greatly increased, and uncustomary subjects like Russian and Asian history had been introduced as contemporary events had emphasized their importance.

In the American field Paul Buck, Arthur, Jr., and Oscar Handlin were full professors, with Frank Freidel and Donald H. Fleming presently to be added from other institutions; and Bernard Bailyn and Ernest R. May were moving to the top from within the Department.

I settled readily into my new groove, happily relinquishing the routine of classes, committees, and examinations. I continued to occupy my Widener study, but, as earlier, did most of my work at home, being at my desk usually from nine in the morning till six in the afternoon with a break for lunch. I also attended, though less regularly, the weekly luncheons of the Department, now as an interested spectator of the proceedings without any responsibility for the decisions reached. Elizabeth and I lived on in our Gray Gardens home, and I felt a bit freer than before to spend time caring for the garden. The chief change in our manner of life, and one we regretted, was the dropping away of the Sunday afternoon teas, for as the graduate students who had worked with me took teaching jobs, there were no new ones to replace them. The old-timers, though, seemed never to return to Cambridge without seeking us out.

I had envisaged retirement as a blessed state in which I would do only what I wanted to do and not what others wanted me to. It soon appeared, however, that even when one has deliberately taken himself out of circulation the old adage holds true: "Eternal vigilance is the price of liberty." Persons and institutions, believing that time must be hanging heavy on my hands, asked me to accept lecture engagements, act as visiting professor, take research positions, and the like. Especially tempting was the invitation to inaugurate a center of American studies at the University of Delhi in India, the kind of project which when I was younger had twice taken me to Europe. Publishers, too, joined in, suggesting books to write which they promised would sell but lacked appeal for me. In all these instances I tried to answer diplomatically but suspect that, in some quarters at least, I earned a reputation for churlishness.

Certain older activities, however, it seemed natural to continue since they took little consecutive time and were well worth while in themselves. Thus I remained on the governing board of Radcliffe College, and in 1959 served on the committee to find a new president, repeating the experience of sixteen years before in helping select Wilbur K. Jordan. We canvassed over a hundred prospects of both sexes, ending up, as we had hoped, with a highly qualified woman. Strangely enough, women, though advancing in nearly every other walk of life, had lost ground in the last ten years as presidents of girls' colleges. The choice of Dean Mary I. Bunting of Douglass College in Rutgers University accordingly assisted in improving the situation. Among Mrs. Bunting's early accomplishments was the transforming of the morganatic marriage with Harvard into a true union. Since 1962 Radcliffe has, without losing its identity or president, formed a unit within the larger institution, with the girls receiving Harvard diplomas. A long trend reached its logical conclusion. My own connection with Radcliffe ceased in mid-1963 after twenty-one years on the Council, and with it my chairmanship of the Advisory Board of the Women's Archives.

To carry out an uncompleted commitment, I continued as one of the five advisers on the preparation of a history of the United States government's activities in science, a project instituted in 1953 by the National Science Foundation. This pioneering venture, directed by A. Hunter Dupree, one of my PhD.'s, eventuated in 1957 in the publication of his notable work *Science in the Federal Government*, surveying the subject from the beginning to the eve of World War II. Unexpectedly I also became active again on the National Historical Publications Commission. Eisenhower, it will be remembered, had not reappointed me, but President Kennedy returned me to it in 1961 when the first vacancy occurred.

In addition, I have kept up attendance at meetings of the American Historical Association as well as of various local historical societies. The national gatherings afforded an opportunity of seeing old friends, making new ones among the younger men, and re-establishing association with former students. To learn of their progress in teaching and research and of their future plans has been a source of unending satisfaction. At the December convention in 1957 in New York a group of them and their wives honored Elizabeth and me with a dinner in anticipation of my seventieth birthday. It was an occasion to warm any teacher's heart.

Besides these prior associations I became involved in two new undertakings. One was the promotion, for purposes of historical study, of a conception of education unlike that traditionally in vogue. This formulation broadened the term beyond knowledge communicated in the classroom to all the myriad influences, in and out of school, which develop young people's mental powers and skills and outlook on life. Education so understood would, for example, explain the riddle otherwise presented by such towering figures as Benjamin Franklin and Abraham Lincoln, who had received next to no formal instruction. A natural enough point of view for the social historian, it diverged sharply from that of the men in colleges of education, who had hitherto dominated the subject. In 1955 the Fund for the Advancement of Education appointed a committee under Paul Buck to spread the conception. Among the members, besides myself, were Richard J. Storr of the University of Chicago and Timothy L. Smith of the University of Minnesota, two more of my Ph.D.'s. The committee has held conferences of interested scholars, made grants for exploring portions of the field or preparing courses in it, and helped librarians gather needed source materials. A conference held jointly with the Institute of Early American History and Culture resulted in 1960 in an influential book by the principal speaker, Bernard Bailyn, *Education in the Forming of*

American Society: Needs and Opportunities for Study. Inquiries equally promising are in prospect for the national period.

The other new enterprise lay far afield from my previous concerns but appealed to me both as a historian and as a citizen. This was a thoroughgoing study of the status of the American Indian in relation to the dominant society. I had long been interested in the role of the immigrant in our history, but here was a people to whom all the rest of us were immigrants. They had suffered terribly at our hands since earliest days, and the various attempts at peaceful assimilation, from the well-intentioned General Allotment Act of 1887 onward, had sadly miscarried. In 1953 Congress, impatient at being further plagued with the problem and pressed by white groups seeking valuable timber, mineral, water, or other natural resources, decreed that all remaining reservations should be terminated "as rapidly as possible." This declaration affected some 300,000 men, women, and children in over 300 federally administered communities, largely in the trans-Mississippi West. Most of the tribes, dwelling on infertile land, were destitute. Others, possessing undeveloped economic means, had no desire or lacked the training to abandon their immemorial mode of life. It was usually a minority of a band who were eager as well as competent to strike out for themselves. Should the government act precipitately and without the full co-operation and adequate preparation of those concerned, the result could only be to cast many of the race within a few years onto relief rolls.

It was this situation which prompted the Fund for the Republic early in 1957 to set up the Commission on the Rights, Liberties and Responsibilities of the American Indian under President O. Meredith Wilson of the University of Oregon (later of the University of Minnesota) as chairman. The other members, in addition to myself, were William W. Keeler, chief of the Cherokee Nation and an executive of the Phillips Petroleum Company in Oklahoma, Karl N. Llewellyn of the University of Chicago Law School, and Charles A. Sprague, publisher of the *Oregon Statesman* at Salem. To learn about conditions at first hand we visited in particular Oregon (where the Klamaths were on the point of being terminated), New Mexico and Arizona (the states with the highest concentration of red men), and Oklahoma (where assimilation had gone farthest), conferring with tribal leaders, local officials of the Federal Bureau of Indian Affairs, and representatives of the states concerned.

To me all this proved an illuminating if depressing experience. At a meeting of the tribal council of the Pueblo of Taos in New Mexico, to cite one example, a grim-visaged oldster, speaking through an interpreter, sternly reproached the United States government for helping underdeveloped peoples overseas while neglecting similar responsibilities to red citizens within its own borders. My education proceeded a step further when I partook of barbecued buffalo at a convention of the National Congress of American Indians in Claremore, Oklahoma, and discovered that this was also the first time most of the delegates had ever tasted it. This meat had, of course, been the mainstay of the Plains Indians until white hunters decimated the herds. On still another occasion an elder on the San Carlos Apache Reservation in Arizona related with pride that the tribe was planning to solve the vexing problem of keeping their boys out of mischief in the summertime by introducing Boy Scout troops. This resort to an expedient which the white man had himself borrowed from the Indians seemed the ultimate irony. As in so many other cases, the band was poised between two ways of life without being firmly rooted in either.

To supplement the field excursions a research staff in Albuquerque, New Mexico, examined all the relevant existing literature, official and unofficial, and engaged specialists to prepare reports in depth on particular subjects such as Indian education, health and medical care, economic resources, tribal government, and the recently adopted program of piecemeal relocation. In January, 1961, the Commission published a short preliminary report in the hope of influencing the policies of the incoming Washington administration; and President Kennedy, through the Secretary of the Interior, named a committee of his own which, under our fellow member Keeler as chairman, endorsed the Commission's major findings and recommendations. The new program aims at terminating reservations only when the tribesmen are properly equipped to move into the mainstream of American life and desire to do so. "Lo, the poor Indian," may yet become just a quotation from Alexander Pope's "Essay on Man." The Commission's comprehensive report has yet to appear.

These various activities loom larger in the telling than in the actual amount of time consumed. It is even possible that the interruptions sharpened my mind for work at my desk. In all honesty, however, extraneous incentives have never seemed necessary; scholarship itself has proved infinitely stimulating. The first book I undertook after retirement emanated from an interest formed many years before while toiling on my doctoral thesis. Despite the voluminous writings on the Revolutionary movement in the interval none had depicted the role of the press in arousing and uniting the colonists. Between 1935 and 1941 I had published articles on aspects of the subject, but other projects plus the need for additional research had prevented a thoroughgoing treatment. Now, with more time at my disposal, *Prelude to Independence: The Newspaper War on Britain, 1764-1776*, appeared in January, 1958. Out of the wealth of the material I had preceded it with articles on several neglected collateral topics: "Liberty Tree, a Genealogy," in the *New England Quarterly*, 1952; "A Note on Songs as Patriot Propaganda," in the *William and Mary Quarterly*, 1954; and "Political Mobs and the American Revolution," in the *Proceedings* of the American Philosophical Society, 1956.

At the urging of publishers who wished to reprint certain standard works in the colonial field I also provided introductions for J. Franklin Jameson's *The American Revolution Considered as a Social Movement* (1956), Herbert L. Osgood's *The American Colonies in the Eighteenth Century* (1958), Edward Eggleston's *The Transit of Civilization to America in the Seventeenth Century* (1959), and Carl Becker's *The History of Political Parties in the Province of New York, 1760-1776* (1960). In each case there was a compelling reason, for, except retrospectively, I did not consider myself a colonial historian. Osgood, who died in 1918, had inducted me into my lifework; Jameson until his death in 1937 had been the elder statesman of the profession; Becker, who passed away in 1945, had been both consulting editor of the *History of American Life* and friend; and Eggleston, though belonging to an earlier generation than the three others, dying in 1902, seemed to me the unrecognized but real father of American social history. His example had had no effect only because he had been far ahead of his time. Over a decade before James Harvey Robinson, he had coined the expression "The New History" in his presidential address to the American Historical Association in 1900. In my introduction to the volume I sought to restore this novelist-turned-historian to his rightful position.

An invitation to give an address at Bucknell University in 1957 on the occasion of receiving an honorary degree led to an article on "America's Influence: Our Ten Contributions to Civilization," published in the *Atlantic Monthly* in 1959 and incorporated in a new edition of *Paths to the Present* four years later. Curiously enough, the theme was one historians had never before written about, but, aside from that, it seemed timely in view of America's rise to leadership of the free world. Letters from readers evidenced that the moment was ripe for such an affirmative exposition. Owing to the fumbling policies of the Eisenhower administration at home and abroad and the alarming advances of the Soviet Union in science and technology, many Americans had lost a sense of national purpose and craved a rebaptism of faith in their birthright, particularly in its spiritual and ideological values. The essay has been reprinted in a variety of anthologies for college use and translated by the United States Information Agency for distribution in Germany, Japan, South Vietnam, and elsewhere.

Since the writing of *Prelude to Independence* most of my time, however, has been devoted to a multivolume history of the social and cultural development of the American people. The groundwork for it already existed in the course I had long given, but there were many phases of the subject I wished to probe more deeply, and this has entailed considerable additional research as well as reflection. Consequently progress on the work has proved slow; the first volume is still under way. As a sort of trial flight, however, a fragment on "The Aristocracy in Colonial America" is soon to appear in the *Proceedings* of the Massachusetts Historical Society.

Beyond the call of professional duty I retained an interest in public affairs, though now somewhat more in the role of an onlooker. Eisenhower, the justly renowned general of World War II, operated in the presidency after the manner of a McKinley or Taft, each of whom, however, the seventy-five historians were to rate above him as chief executive. Like these predecessors he believed essentially in negative government. He had, moreover, filled the key cabinet posts with men recruited from corporate business and finance and, perhaps because of his prior unacquaintance with civilian problems, deferred in crucial matters to their judgment. Within my own memory as a voter, however, there had been commanding figures in the White House like Woodrow Wilson and the two Roosevelts, so that Eisenhower, as responsible head of the government during a critical stage of the Cold War, seemed to fall sadly short of the nation's needs. That, however, was not the view of most citizens, who still beheld him in heroic proportions and attributed to him the peace and plenty the country enjoyed. In running against him in 1956 Stevenson faced insuperable odds and in any event proved less effective in presenting his cause than in his first contest. Arthur, Jr., was again in Stevenson's entourage, with the national ADA renewing its support of 1952 and the Massachusetts branch doing everything possible to help. But Eisenhower polled more popular and electoral votes than before, repeating his victory in Massachusetts as well.

The 1960 presidential race, with Stevenson out of consideration, found me in the camp of Hubert H. Humphrey for the Democratic candidacy. The Minnesotan had been an outstanding liberal Senator, and few men in government were so widely and deeply informed. I helped organize the Massachusetts Volunteers for Humphrey, but when he was outdistanced by Kennedy in the primaries, it was easy to switch allegiance to my fellow Bay Stater. Kennedy had grown steadily in statesmanlike stature after entering the Senate, and his speeches both before and after his nomination demonstrated forward-looking convictions on domestic and international questions. In no event could I have voted for the Republican contender, Nixon, whose public career had excited my profound distrust. His television debates with Kennedy only underscored the feeling. Arthur, a friend of Kennedy's since college days, served him in the same capacity he earlier had Stevenson. The national ADA again endorsed the Democratic ticket, but the local chapter's support was hardly needed to help carry Massachusetts for its native son. Though he won nationally only by a hairbreadth in the popular vote, his electoral majority was quite decisive, and the issue raised in 1928 by Al Smith's Catholicism seemed at last to be laid to rest.

Ralph McGill of the Atlanta *Constitution*, discussing the outcome in his syndicated column, believed that what he called the "Political Law of Arthur Schlesinger the Elder" had been "basic in the Democratic victory." James Reston in advance of the election had written in the New York *Times* that

Kennedy, "well aware of this doctrine, . . . has based his campaign on the assumption." Actually, the cycle theory timed the recession from conservatism for 1962, "with a possible margin of a year or two in one direction or the other." Had the new captain taken command a little too soon to profit from the liberal swing? If the theory is valid, his difficulties with a Congress of his own party suggest as much. Arthur joined the regime as a special assistant to the President, and two other White House aides, as well as three cabinet officers and a goodly number of major administrators, were ADA members or associates.

In the latter portion of this narrative Thomas, my younger son, has been lost sight of after returning from World War II. The reason for this is that upon graduating from Brown in 1946 Tom's career took him away from Cambridge and involved him less directly in family activities. Working as a newspaper reporter successively in Spartanburg, S.C., Charlotte, N.C., and on the Washington *Post*, he shifted in 1951 to the State Department to edit a fortnightly bulletin summarizing for the general public current international developments. But the advent of the Republicans to power in 1953 abruptly severed the connection, and he joined the administrative staff of Colonial Williamsburg, where he has been ever since. One of his responsibilities is to organize an annual conference for foreign students in United States universities about to return home. For three days they listen to speakers representing business, labor, literature, the fine arts, and other fields present an over-all picture of American civilization. When I was on the panel in 1958 the questions and comments kept me very much on my toes. Tom as a youngster had vowed he would never follow his father in becoming a historian, so it was with some amusement that we saw him, in spite of himself, winding up in a historical calling, though one concerned, of course, with the three-dimensional remains of the past rather than the written documents. Moreover, on the side, he teaches extension classes in international relations and comparative government for the College of William and Mary. Every summer during his vacation we visit him and his family at their delightful cottage at Sandbridge on the Virginia shore.

There is also more to say about Elizabeth. Despite her repeated appearances in these pages her place in the total story has not received full justice. She has run the household with an unobtrusive efficiency which freed me for maximum time at my desk and, by the same token, has stood guard against undue outside interruptions. Her unfailing interest and encouragement have furthermore sustained my research and writing, and everything I have printed has first been subjected to her critical eye. Besides, she has performed scholarly work on her own. Her articles, published in such periodicals as the *New England Quarterly*, the *New-York Historical Society Quarterly*, the *Harvard Library Bulletin*, and *American Heritage*, fill in some of the many gaps of knowledge regarding the position of women and children in American society from colonial days onward. Esthetically, too, she has been a force. Her pleasure in flowers has not only expressed itself in the garden but in lending color and beauty to our home in all seasons of the year. A devoted mother, she gave increasing attention as the boys grew older to community activities, some of which have here been noted far too briefly. But, above everything else, there has been our life together, enriched by the joy and satisfaction afforded by our sons and their families. Next year, through it seems impossible that the time could have passed so swiftly, we will reach the golden anniversary of our marriage.

XI

Some Reflections

People have asked me what my attitude is toward religion and why I have always held liberal political and social opinions. Younger members of my profession have wondered about the changes that have occurred in the theory and practice of history during my lifetime. The answers to these queries are to a large extent implicit in what has already been set down, but perhaps some elaboration may not be amiss.

The religion of a sensible man, someone has remarked, is the religion a sensible man never talks about. That is especially true of me, because where a belief in God is concerned I have, in Max Weber's expression, been "unmusical." Probably this originated in youthful reaction to the ostentatious sanctity displayed at revivals, which was so often followed by quiet backsliding. At any rate, as far back as my memory goes I have thought of goodness—or godliness, to use the pious term —as a product purely of conscience and have regarded that indispensable monitor as the resultant of many conditioning factors, of which religious faith or affiliation may or may not be one. On this score it follows that the temperament and circumstances of the individual determine whether his peace of mind arises from the teachings of Holy Writ or from personal assessment of the values of life or from some other source. What is essential is that people, whatever their spiritual motivation, should strive to act on right impulses for decent and humane ends. Consequently the question of the existence of a Supreme Being has not seemed important, nor by the same token has the prospect of a future state of rewards and punishments. You live but once, and if you leave the world a little better or have sincerely tried to do so, once is enough. If there should be a hereafter, it will come regardless of one's religious professions, and a just God will see that the rewards and punishments fit the manner of life that has been led.

Nothing has puzzled me more in the case of religious adherents than the grief manifested at funerals. Should not the devout, instead of bemoaning the loss of a loved one, rejoice that he has left behind worldly trials and attained eternal bliss? Paul Laurence Dunbar has unforgettably voiced the feeling of the departed:

> When all is done, and my last word is said,
> And ye who loved me murmur, "He is dead,"
> Let no one weep, for fear that I should know,
> And sorrow too that ye should sorrow so.

When I told the poet Robert Frost a few years ago that I was uninterested in the ultimate meaning of life he strongly demurred. In matters of this order, he maintained, no person has the right to be neutral; he must either acknowledge a Divine Power or declare himself an atheist; agnosticism is no tenable middle ground. But if this view is correct—which I do not concede—the adopting of one or the other of the extreme positions would not, to the best of my knowledge, have altered my own actions or outlook on life. Had I joined any religious denomination it would have been the Unitarians, because of their central concern with ethical conduct. Through the years nearly all my friends among the clergy have been of that persuasion or have shared Unitarian convictions.

My liberalism in secular affairs likewise harks back to childhood. Perhaps it goes back even farther on Justice Brandeis's premise that liberal and conservative tendencies arise largely from genes. Xenia, though a Republican stronghold and conservative in politics, was not a place where one's standing in the community depended on wealth or ancestry or ethnic origin. The Republican boss himself was of German extraction, and he had built up from scratch the town's largest grocery. I remember once telling Father in dismay that some boys at school had bragged they were better Americans than I, since their folks had been in the United States for generations. "You say to them," he laughed, "that when their parents came to America they brought nothing but their bare skins, while I at least had clothes on my back. And tell them, too, that their parents had no choice in the matter but that your father came because he wanted to—because he thought the United States the best country on earth." This twitting by my playmates did not reflect the adult attitude, of course, but the incident left me with lasting pride in being one of the nation's newer citizens. Immigrants, I never afterward forgot, were voluntary Americans, not a chosen people but what seemed better: a choosing people.

My youthful environment thus provided an image of America as a pluralistic society as well as a land of opportunity, and nothing in later life has dimmed the vision. The writings of Jefferson and Emerson, which I came across in college, helped crystallize this conception of human potentialities regardless of race, economic condition, or creed. The great Virginian avowed out of the breadth of his experience, "I am one of those who think well of the human character." He declared, "I steer my bark with Hope in the head, leaving Fear astern. My hopes indeed sometimes fail; but not oftener than the forebodings of the gloomy." The Concord sage emphasized the need of constant watchfulness to safeguard the rights of the many: "What is a man born for but to be a Re-former, a Re-maker of what man has made; a renouncer of lies; a restorer of truth and good. . . ."

The study of history in after years only reinforced the belief that life, liberty, and the pursuit of happiness constitute the birthright of every man and woman and that a government of the people must strive tirelessly to ensure its preservation. This does not imply that every proposed remedy for a social ill should be uncritically adopted, but it does mean that all the avenues of inquiry, suggestion, advocacy, and protest must be kept open, on Jefferson's principle that "error of opinion may be tolerated where reason is left free to combat it." In the academic world, which has sown so many fruitful ideas for the common welfare, it signifies the right of professors to speak fearlessly on issues from specialized knowledge as well as to express convictions outside the classroom as interested citizens, with the correlative right of students to hear and consider conflicting points of view. Academic freedom, as in the case of liberty of the press, is of vital concern not only to the practitioners. In a democratic society it is equally indispensable for offering lawmakers and the electorate alternatives of policy.

As for the scholarly study of American history in the period of my professional career, it has made enormous strides. These rest on the foundations of scientific method laid by the preceding generation, men of the caliber of Osgood, Channing, Andrews, Dunning, and Turner, some of whom in 1884 had helped establish the American Historical Association. Strongly influenced by German precept and example, they sought to reconstruct the past with objectivity; to search out thoroughly, assess critically, and base their findings solidly on firsthand data; and to explain men's acts and attitudes in the light of the conditions of the age and place in which they had lived.

These criteria continued to be the guidelines for the historians of my generation notwithstanding a greater recognition that disciplined insight is sometimes justifiable to bridge gaps in documented knowledge and that the suppression of personal bias is in the absolute sense unattainable. Think of the temptation of the scholar living below the Mason and Dixon Line to write, in the familiar saying, "an impartial history of the Civil War from the Southern standpoint," and I myself have with some justice been called by a Marxist historian an example of "the liberal bourgeois school." The very selection of data from the abundance at hand involves a subjective evaluation of which the investigator may be unconscious, and constant self-appraisal is called for. Like Christianity, which even the dedicated find difficult to practice, objectivity constitutes the ideal for which the conscientious historian steadfastly strives. The measure of success attained by the profession appears in the consensus in regard to the major forces and events in American history. By and large, the differences that persist concern matters of detail—disagreements due generally to the discovery of new source materials or to the customary revolt of younger men against the hard-and-fast views of their elders: the "conventional wisdom," to borrow J. K. Galbraith's term in another connection. All this makes for the growth and health of historical study, and it would be unfortunate for the process ever to stop.

The principal thrust of fresh and contagious interpretations in my years came from Turner and Beard, each rebelling against the views of his time. Both overstated their theses— Turner as to the significance of the frontier and Beard regarding the impact of economic self-interest—but they deemed this essential in order to break through the crust of established conceptions. "The truth is," Turner wrote me in 1922 while I was still at Iowa, "that I found it necessary to hammer pretty hard and pretty steadily on the frontier idea to 'get it in,' as a corrective to the kind of thinking I found some thirty years ago and less." And in similar vein Beard remarked of his future plans after finishing the *Economic Origins of Jeffersonian Democracy*, "I'm going forward with my cutting-out work in the field. I shall rough-hew it all the way, leaving it to others to correct my perspective and many errors and do the balanced job." Each, as a result, has in recent years suffered at the hands of self-styled revisionists who in their zeal have themselves indulged in overstatements. But the Hegelian sequence of thesis, antithesis, and synthesis is already evident, promising the "balanced job" which Beard expected. Ideally it should not prove needful for the pursuit of truth to pass through these three stages, and historical findings have not always had to do so; but in other areas of inquiry as well, the process has led to fuller understanding. Even in the natural sciences, distortion followed by dissent and eventual refining of the original theory has spurred great advances.

No United States historian, however, since Henry Adams early in the century has, like Arnold Toynbee in England, essayed a cosmic interpretation of man's stay on earth or even of that of the American segment of humanity. Professor Geyl when visiting our leading academic centers from coast to coast was surprised at the lack of interest in Toynbee's grandiose conception, the Hollander being himself Toynbee's sharpest critic abroad. Perhaps there is not enough poetry— or theology—in the American historian's make-up for this sort of venture. At any rate, with very few exceptions, he has rejected the very thought of immutable laws in human affairs. Encompassing, simplistic systems go against his grain, since he finds causative factors too complex, as well as too inconstant in nature and intensity, to be reduced to the equivalent, say, of the force of gravity in the physical world. He chooses to explain events in the small rather than in the large and, when more daring, to generalize only in regard to particular lines of development. The interpretative essays in *Paths to the Present*, for example, possess this limited character. But, even so, the cycle theory of government trends, which, as has been seen, aroused the most widespread attention and also accorded with a concept which economists have fruitfully applied to business fluctuations, has not set historians to probing analogous recurrences in other fields of thought and action. Thus, in religion there have been persisting alternations of orthodoxy and heterodoxy, in literature of realism and romanticism, in the fine arts of classicism and experimentalism. Is it not worth inquiring whether these are simply haphazard phenomena or, as may well be possible, expressions of an inherent and explicable rhythm?

American historians, moreover, have devoted little time to airing in print their ideas on the nature of history or writing dissertations on methodology, undertakings common to professionals abroad. Such abstract discussions as have appeared take the form characteristically of papers in learned journals rather than of book-length treatments, as in Europe. I myself, at the juncture when the interrelation of the social sciences was very much to the fore, spoke on the particular role of history at the University of Virginia and the Brookings Institution in lecture series which included representatives of the allied fields. The two groups of addresses were later published respectively as *Research in the Social Sciences* (1929) and *Essays on Research in the Social Sciences* (1931). Obviously matters concerning the meaning of history and the criteria of practice enter indispensably into the historian's labors, but I am probably typical in thinking that a scholar renders his principal service in exemplifying the principles instead of discoursing on them. The proof of the pudding is in the eating.

The most significant development in American historical study has been the enlarging of its base to include the totality of human experience or, in Edward Eggleston's words, the shift from "drum and trumpet history" to "the history of culture, the real history of men and women." After initial resistance by scholars wedded to the simpler and more easily documented political record, the conception made quick headway through the profession, especially among the younger members. The trail blazing of the *History of American Life* undoubtedly facilitated the process. A rough indication of the consequences may be seen by comparing the *Harvard Guide to American History,* which six of us in the History Department brought out in 1954 under Oscar Handlin's editorship, with the Channing, Hart, and Turner *Guide* of 1912, the previously widely used manual. The later work presents an almost brand-new approach to the past in both the range of topics embraced and the variety of source materials cited.

This is not to say that social history has yet issued beyond the stage of trial and error. Much of it is still of the taxonomic or descriptive variety, consisting of catalogues of facts grouped in appropriate categories and treated for their own sake instead of in relation to other developments of the times. [Social history, maturely conceived, seeks to grasp and depict both the inner and outer life of society and to integrate the two, and for this there must be found a unifying theme inferred from a painstaking examination of the data.] This, each volume of the *History of American Life* strove to do with more or less success. A special type of difficulty arises when essential evidence is lacking in the conventional documentation and is only implicit. Original and creative thought springs in every field from some individual mind, but whether the thought influences the age depends in a democratic country on the mental, moral, and emotional make-up of the mass of people. Insofar as these attitudes are not expressly stated, it becomes necessary to extract them from patterns of collective behavior. Obviously today's historian faces odds unknown to, or unacknowledged by, the founders of the scientific school. Every year, however, manifests increasing mastery of the problems.

Aside from subject matter the most striking change has appeared in the improved status of the historian himself. This has resulted, on the one hand, from vastly greater financial encouragement for carrying on original work and, on the other, from opportunities of employment apart from teaching. At the apprenticeship stage university fellowships for research and travel and comparable types of support have multiplied, and they are paralleled by similar and often more liberal subventions from outside sources. Having won his spurs, the historian at an ever larger number of institutions enjoys leaves of absence with pay, as well as help for research on the ground; and foundations, learned bodies, publishing houses, and other agencies provide additional assistance in the form of handsome fellowships, grants-in-aid, prizes, even subsidies for the writing and publishing of manuscripts. To an old-timer the contrast with earlier conditions is somewhat like that between the hair shirt and purple and fine linen, and he may wonder to what extent the increased incentives have paid off. Unquestionably they have accelerated projects which would otherwise have taken longer to complete, and they have doubtless swelled the total scholarly output. But, in the light of present evidence at least, they have effected no "knowledge explosion" in the historical field. As yet no pregnant contributions comparable to those of an Eggleston or Turner or Beard have come to view.

From the standpoint of employment the trained historian finds many alternative openings outside university walls. One widening avenue is the administration of historical societies, archives and museums, historic houses, outdoor restorations, and historically famous sites. Another is the ongoing work of military and civilian branches of the federal government in historical research and publication, particularly notable since World War II, and the similar activity of important business corporations. Still another is the editing of the collected papers of statesmen, exemplified in recent years by the scholarly volumes containing the writings of Jefferson, Franklin, the Adams family, and Hamilton, with many like projects planned or in course of execution. These are all outlets calling for high professional ability and possess the appeal of spreading knowledge of the American past to a far larger audience than that in the classroom.

If I were to be given the opportunity of living my life anew, I hope that without benefit of hindsight I would have the wisdom to choose again the career of historian. No other could have afforded greater personal satisfaction. In it one deals not with the dead bones of the past, as is sometimes alleged, but with its life-giving spirit. In words as true now as when written in the seventeenth century the Englishman John Dunton observed,

History has been call'd, by a great Man, *Speculum Mundi*: The Looking-Glass of the World; It gives the best prospect into Humane Affairs, and makes us familiar with the remotest Regions: by this we safely sit in our Closets, and view the horrid Devastations of Countreys, Tumults, Changes and Ruptures of Common-Wealths; The Reverse of Fortunes, the Religions, Politicks and Governments of Foreign Nations; by this we may consult what practices have Establish'd Kingdoms, what laws have render'd any particular Nations more Safe, happy and Civiliz'd than its Neighbours; and what has Contributed to the Weakness and Overthrow of Bodies-Politick; and, in a Prospect of the Whole, a New Scheme may be drawn, for future Ages to act by.

He does not assert, it will be noticed, that a knowledge of history makes it possible to predict what is yet to happen, only that by revealing bygone failures and successes it suggests the means by which men can act more intelligently when problems arise. It places them in the continuing stream of thought, institutions, and events. In the case of the scholar, moreover, it provides the basic ingredient of all departments of learning. Whether it be art or science, philosophy, literature, or economics, the accumulation of data, insights, and skills through the ages underlies the current state of attainment. By extending the collective human memory history thus saves us from being prisoners of the present.

For the student of United States history there is in addition the special joy of discovering and understanding how one's own people have reached their present condition; why, as somebody has said, we have come to behave like Americans. The story contains elements both heartening and tragic inasmuch as it involves, in Emerson's words, incessant "comparison of the idea with the fact"—the ineradicable idea or ideal being the "infinite worthiness in man." One learns, too, how fortunately delusive has been the much-mouthed phrase "splendid isolation." Despite the width of the ocean America has from the beginning adopted or adapted Old World principles of government and ways of life and, alternatively, has held up a lamp to Europe and, more recently, to Asia and Africa. It has also uniquely provided a home for men and women of other lands.

This record of things once thought and wrought should reassure us in facing the troubled times which now prevail. The United States as a "nation of nations"—Walt Whitman's phrase—dramatically evinces the underlying unity of mankind, the triumph in a free society of men's inborn likenesses over their acquired differences, and thereby foreshadows a world in which the force of law will replace the law of force. The perils of the moment, however appalling, should not engender despair. They should, on the contrary, evoke renewed determination to set humanity once again, and this time more securely, on the path to freedom, peace, and justice for all.

Index

Academic freedom, at Ohio State, 60; at Iowa, 64-65; at Harvard, 92, 94-96, 100-01, 122; importance of, 103, 196

Advisory Committee on Records, of War Administration, 142-43

American as Reformer, The, 115-16

American Defense, Harvard Group, 139, 141, 142

American Historical Association, meetings of, 53, 55, 74, 112, 113, 119, 120-22, 184; prizes of, 54, 69, 91

American history, at Ohio State, 21, 37, 49; at Columbia, 36-37; at Iowa, 68, 72; at Harvard, 75, 77-78, 88-92; summary of trends in, 113, 180, 196-200; in England, 166-67; in Holland, 172-73; in Belgium, 174; in Sweden and Norway, 175-76

Americans for Democratic Action, founded, 147-48; in Massachusetts, 148, 153, 190; in Kennedy administration, 191

Andrews, Charles M., on *Colonial Merchants,* 54; visits University of Iowa, 70; and Colonial Williamsburg, 120; as historian, 196

Bancroft, Elizabeth, 22, 33, 41, 42, 43, 44, 45, 56; at Ohio State, 30, 31; visits New York, 39-40; marries, 51-52. *See also* Schlesinger, Elizabeth B.

Beard, Charles A., 43, 112, 157; characterized, 35; on *Colonial Merchants,* 53-54; meets Turner, 55; on economic interpretation of history, 198, 201

Becker, Carl, as consulting editor, 72, 111-12; as author, 105-06, 188; as stylist, 117

Bowser, Lizzie, 10, 16

Brandeis, Louis D., 124-26, 195

Brandt, Walther I., on Iowa faculty, 68

Bridenbaugh, Carl, 91, 121

Brown, Ira V., wins award, 91

Bryan, William Jennings, in 1896 campaign, 16; in 1908 campaign, 28; in 1912 campaign, 42, 43

Buck, Paul H., 91, 95, 99, 182, 184

Bunting, Mary I., president of Radcliffe, 183

Cambridge, Mass., described, 76-77, 79; schools, 80-81

Censoring of history textbooks, 102, 104-06